THE HEART OF MAN

Its Genius for Good and Evil

By Erich Fromm

THE ART OF LOVING

BEYOND THE CHAINS OF ILLUSION

DOGMA OF CHRIST

ESCAPE FROM FREEDOM

THE FORGOTTEN LANGUAGE

MAN FOR HIMSELF

MARX'S CONCEPT OF MAN

MAY MAN PREVAIL?

PSYCHOANALYSIS AND RELIGION

THE SANE SOCIETY

SIGMUND FREUD'S MISSION

SOCIALIST HUMANISM

YOU SHALL BE AS GODS

ZEN BUDDHISM AND PSYCHOANALYSIS

THE HEART OF MAN

Its Genius for Good and Evil

by Erich Fromm

HARPER COLOPHON BOOKS

HARPER & ROW, PUBLISHERS

New York, Evanston, and London

This Colophon paperback edition reprints Volume XII of the RELIGIOUS PER-
SPECTIVES, which is planned and edited by RUTH NANDA ANSHEN. Dr. Anshen's
Epilogue to this reprint appears on page 135.

First HARPER COLOPHON edition published 1968 by Harper & Row, Publishers.

LIBRARY OF CONGRESS CATALOG CARD NUMBER: 64-18053

CONTENTS

Foreword

This book takes up thoughts which were presented in some of my earlier books, and attempts to develop them further. In *Escape from Freedom* I dealt with the problem of freedom and with sadism, masochism, and destructiveness; in the meantime clinical experience and theoretical speculation have led me to what I think is a deeper understanding of freedom as well as of various kinds of aggression and destructiveness. I have been able to distinguish between various kinds of aggression which directly or indirectly are in the service of life, and that malignant form of destructiveness, necrophilia, which is a true love of death as opposed to biophilia which is the love of life. In *Man for Himself* I discussed the problem of ethical norms based on our knowledge of the nature of man, and not on revelation and man-made laws and conventions. In this book I pursue the problem further and discuss the nature of evil and of the choice between good and evil. Finally, this book is in some respects a counterpart to *The Art of Loving*. While the main topic there was man's capacity to love, the main topic here is his capacity to destroy, his narcissism and his incestuous fixation. Yet while the discussion of nonlove fills most pages, the problem of love is also taken up in a new and broader sense, namely, love of life. I try to show that love of life, independence, and the overcoming of narcissism form a "syndrome of growth" as against the "syndrome of decay" formed by love of death, incestuous symbiosis, and malignant narcissism.

I have been led to the pursuit of the study of this syndrome of decay not only on the basis of clinical experience but also by the social and political development of the past years. Ever more pressing becomes the question why, in spite of good will and knowledge of the facts about the consequences of nuclear war, the attempts to avoid it are feeble in comparison with the magnitude of the danger and the likelihood of war, given the continuation of the nuclear-arms race and the continuation of the cold war. This concern has led me to study the phenomenon of indifference to life in an ever increasingly mechanized industrialism, in which man is transformed into a thing, and as a result, is filled with anxiety and with indifference to, if not with hate against, life. But aside from that, the present-day mood of violence which is manifested in juvenile delinquency as well as in the asassination of President John F. Kennedy, demands explanation and understanding as a first possible step toward change. The question arises whether we are headed for a new barbarism—even without the occurrence of nuclear war—or whether a renaissance of our humanist tradition is possible.

Aside from the problems mentioned thus far it is the aim of this book to clarify the relation of my psychoanalytic concepts to Freud's theories. I have never been satisfied with being classified as belonging to a new "school" of psychoanalysis whether it is called the "cultural school" or "Neo-Freudianism." I believe that many of these new schools, while developing valuable insights, have also lost much of the most important discoveries of Freud. I am certainly not an "orthodox Freudian." In fact, any theory which does not change within sixty years is, by this very fact, no longer the same as the original theory of the master; it is a fossilized repetition, and by being a repetition it is actually a deformation. Freud's basic discoveries were conceived in a certain philosophical frame of reference, that of the mechanistic materialism current among most natural scientists at the beginning of this century. I believe that the further development of Freud's thought requires a different philosophical frame of reference, that of *dialectic humanism*. I try to show in this book that Freud's greatest discoveries, that of the Oedipus complex, narcissism, and the death instinct, were hobbled by his philosophical premises and that, freed from them and translated into a new frame of reference, Freud's findings become ever more potent and meaningful.[1] I believe that it is the frame of reference of humanism, of its paradoxical blend of relentless criticism, uncompromising realism, and rational faith which will permit the fruitful development of the work for which Freud laid the foundations.

One more remark: While the thoughts expressed in this book are all the result of my clinical work as a psychoanalyst (and to some extent as a student of social processes), I have omitted much of the clinical documentation. This documentation I plan to offer in a larger work which will deal with the theory and therapy of humanist psychoanalysis.

Lastly, I want to express my indebtedness to Paul Edwards for his critical suggestions in respect to the chapter on Freedom, Determinism, Alternativism.

ERICH FROMM

---

[1] I want to emphasize that this concept of psychoanalysis does not imply replacing Freud's theory by what is now known as "existentialist analysis." This substitute for Freud's theory is often shallow, using words taken from Heidegger or Sartre (or Husserl) without connecting them with serious penetration of clinical facts. This holds true for some "existentialist" psychoanalysts as well as for Sartre's psychological thinking which though brilliant is nevertheless superficial and without sound clinical basis. Sartre's, like Heidegger's, existentialism is not a new beginning, but an end; they are the expression of the despair of Western man after the catastrophe of two world wars, and after Hitler's and Stalin's regimes; but they are not only the expression of despair. They are the manifestations of an extreme bourgeois egotism and solipsism. This is easier to understand if we deal with a philosopher like Heidegger who sympathized with Nazism. It is more deceptive in Sartre's case, who claims to represent Marxist thought and to be the philosopher of the future; he is nevertheless the exponent of the spirit of the society of *anomie* and selfishness which he criticizes and wants to change. As to the belief that life has no meaning given and guaranteed by God, many systems have held this belief; among the religions, prominently Buddhism. However, in their claim that there are no objective values valid for all men, and in his concept of freedom which amounts to egotistic arbitrariness, Sartre and his followers lose the most important achievement of theistic and nontheistic religion, as well as of the humanist tradition.

THE HEART OF MAN

Its Genius for Good and Evil

I
Man—Wolf or Sheep?

There are many who believe that men are sheep; there are others who believe that men are wolves. Both sides can muster good arguments for their positions. Those who propose that men are sheep have only to point to the fact that men are easily influenced to do what they are told, even if it is harmful to themselves; that they have followed their leaders into wars which brought them nothing but destruction; that they have believed any kind of nonsense if it was only presented with sufficient vigor and supported by power—from the harsh threats of priests and kings to the soft voices of the hidden and not-so-hidden persuaders. It seems that the majority of men are suggestible, half-awake children, willing to surrender their will to anyone who speaks with a voice that is threatening or sweet enough to sway them. Indeed, he who has a conviction strong enough to withstand the opposition of the crowd is the exception rather than the rule, an exception often admired centuries later, mostly laughed at by his contemporaries.

It is on this assumption—that men are sheep—that the Great Inquisitors and the dictators have built their systems. More than that, this very belief that men are sheep and hence need leaders to make the decisions for them, has often given the leaders the sincere conviction that they were fulfilling a moral duty—even though a tragic one—if they gave man what he wanted: if they were leaders who took away from him the burden of responsibility and freedom.

17

But if most men have been sheep, why is it that man's life is so different from that of sheep? His history has been written in blood; it is a history of continuous violence, in which almost invariably force has been used to bend his will. Did Talaat Pasha alone exterminate millions of Armenians? Did Hitler alone exterminate millions of Jews? Did Stalin alone exterminate millions of political enemies? These men were not alone; they had thousands of men who killed for them, tortured for them, and who did so not only willingly but with pleasure. Do we not see man's inhumanity to man everywhere—in ruthless warfare, in murder and rape, in the ruthless exploitation of the weaker by the stronger, and in the fact that the sighs of the tortured and suffering creature have so often fallen on deaf ears and hardened hearts? All these facts have led thinkers like Hobbes to the conclusion that *homo homini lupus* (man is a wolf to his fellow man); they have led many of us today to the assumption that man is vicious and destructive by nature, that he is a killer who can be restrained from his favorite pastime only by fear of more powerful killers.

Yet the arguments of both sides leave us puzzled. It is true that we may personally know some potential or manifest killers and sadists as ruthless as Stalin and Hitler were; yet these are the exceptions rather than the rule. Should we assume that you and I and most average men are wolves in sheep's clothing, and that our "true nature" will become apparent once we rid ourselves of those inhibitions which until now have prevented us from acting like beasts? This assumption is hard to disprove, yet it is not entirely convincing. There are numerous opportunities for cruelty and sadism in everyday life in which people could indulge without fear of retaliation; yet many do not do so; in fact, many react with a certain sense of revulsion when they meet cruelty and sadism.

Is there, then, another and perhaps better explanation for the puzzling contradiction we deal with here? Should we assume that the simple answer is that there is a minority of wolves living side by side with a majority of sheep? The wolves want to kill; the sheep want to follow. Hence the wolves get the sheep to kill, to murder, and to strangle, and the sheep comply not because they enjoy it, but because they want to follow; and even then the killers have to invent stories about the nobility of their cause, about defense against the threat to freedom, about revenge for bayoneted children, raped women, and violated honor, to get the majority of the sheep to act like wolves. This answer sounds plausible, but it still leaves many doubts. Does it not imply that there are two human races, as it were—that of wolves and that of sheep? Furthermore, how is it that sheep can be so easily persuaded to act like wolves if it is not in their nature to do so, even providing that violence is presented to them as a sacred duty? Our assumption regarding wolves and sheep may not be tenable; is it perhaps true after all that the wolves represent the essential quality of human nature, only more overtly than the majority show it? Or, after all, maybe the entire alternative is erroneous. Maybe man is both wolf *and* sheep—or neither wolf *nor* sheep?

The answer to these questions is of crucial importance today, when nations contemplate the use of the most destructive forces for the extinction of their "enemies," and seem not to be deterred even by the possibility that they themselves may be extinguished in the holocaust. If we are convinced that human nature is inherently prone to destroy, that the need to use force and violence is rooted in it, then our resistance to ever increasing brutalization will become weaker and weaker. Why resist the wolves when we are *all* wolves, although some more so than others?

The question whether man is wolf or sheep is only a special formulation of a question which, in its wider and more general aspects, has been one of the most basic problems of Western theological and philosophical thought: Is man basically evil and corrupt, or is he basically good and perfectable? The Old Testament does not take the position of man's fundamental corruption. Adam and Eve's *disobedience* to God are not called sin; nowhere is there a hint that this disobedience has corrupted man. On the contrary, the disobedience is the condition for man's self-awareness, for his capacity to choose, and thus in the last analysis this first act of disobedience is man's first step toward freedom. It seems that their disobedience was even within God's plan; for, according to prophetic thought, man just *because* he was expelled from Paradise is able to make his own history, to develop his human powers, and to attain a new harmony with man and nature as a fully developed individual instead of the former harmony in which he was *not yet* an individual. The Messianic concept of the prophets certainly implies that man is not fundamentally corrupt and that he can be saved without any special act of God's grace. But it does not imply that this potential for good will necessarily win. If man does evil he becomes more evil. Thus, Pharaoh's heart "hardens" because he keeps on doing evil; it hardens to a point where no more change or repentance is possible. The Old Testament offers at least as many examples of evil-doing as of right-doing, and does not exempt even exalted figures like King David from the list of evil doers. The Old Testament view is that man has both capacities—that of good and that of evil—and that man must choose between good and evil, blessing and curse, life and death. Even God does not interfere in his choice; he helps by sending his messengers, the prophets, to teach the norms which lead to the realization of goodness, to identify the evil, and to warn and to protest. But this being done, man is left alone with his "two strivings," that for good and that for evil, and the decision is his alone.

The Christian development was different. In the course of the development of the Christian Church, Adam's disobedience was conceived as sin. In fact, as a sin so severe that it corrupted his nature and with it that of all his descendants, and thus man by his own effort could never rid himself of this corruption. Only God's own act of grace, the appearance of Christ, who died for man, could extinguish man's corruption and offer salvation for those who accepted Christ.

But the dogma of original sin was by no means unopposed in the Church. Pelagius assailed it but was defeated. The Renaissance humanists within the Church tended to weaken it, even though they could not directly assail or deny it, while many heretics did just that. Luther had, if anything, an even more radical view of man's innate evilness and corruption, while thinkers of the Renaissance and later of the Enlightenment took a drastic step in the opposite direction. The latter claimed that all evil in man was nothing but the result of circumstances, hence that man did not really have to choose. Change the circumstances that produce evil, so they thought, and man's original goodness will come forth almost automatically. This view also colored the thinking of Marx and his successors. The belief in man's goodness was the result of man's new self-confidence, gained as a result of the tremendous economic and political progress which started with the Renaissance. Conversely, the moral bankruptcy of the West which began with the First World War and led beyond Hitler and Stalin, Coventry and Hiroshima to the present preparation for universal extinction, brought forth again the traditional emphasis on man's propensity for evil. This new emphasis was a healthy antidote to the underestimation of the inherent potential of evil in man—but too often it served to ridicule those who had not lost their faith in man, sometimes by misunderstanding and even distorting their position.

As one whose views have often been misrepresented as underestimating the potential of evil within man, I want to emphasize that such sentimental optimism is not the mood of my thought. It would be difficult indeed for anyone who has had a long clinical experience as a psychoanalyst to belittle the destructive forces within man. In severely sick patients, he sees these forces at work and experiences the enormous difficulty of stopping them or of channeling their energy into constructive directions. It would be equally difficult for any person who has witnessed the explosive outburst of evil and destructivness since the beginning of the First World War not to see the power and intensity of human destructiveness. Yet there exists the danger that the sense of powerlessness which grips people today—intellectuals as well as the average man—with ever increasing force, may lead them to accept a new version of corruption and original sin which serves as a rationalization for the defeatist view that war cannot be avoided because it is the result of the destructiveness of human nature. Such a view, which sometimes prides itself on its exquisite realism, is unrealistic on two grounds. First, the intensity of destructive strivings by no means implies that they are invincible or even dominant. The second fallacy in this view lies in the premise that wars are primarily the result of psychological forces. It is hardly necessary to dwell long on this fallacy of "psychologism" in the understanding of social and political phenomena. Wars are the result of the decision of political, military, and business leaders to wage war for the sake of gaining territory, natural resources, advantages in trade; for defense against real or alleged threats to their country's security by another power; or for reason of the enhancement of their own personal prestige and glory. These men are not different from the average man: they are selfish, with little capacity to renounce personal advantage for the sake of others; but they are neither cruel nor vicious. When such men—who in ordinary life probably would do more good than harm—get into positions of power where they can command millions of people and control the most destructive weapons, they can cause immense harm. In civilian life they might have destroyed a competitor; in our world of powerful and sovereign states ("sovereign" means not subject to any moral law which restricts the action of the sovereign state), they may destroy the human race. *The ordinary man with extraordinary power* is the chief danger for mankind —not the fiend or the sadist. But just as one needs weapons in order to fight a war, one needs the passions of hate, indignation, destructiveness, and fear in order to get millions of people to risk their lives and to become murderers. These passions are necessary conditions for the waging of war; they are not its causes, any more than guns and bombs by themselves are causes of wars. Many observers have commented that nuclear war differs in this respect from traditional war. The man who will press the buttons sending off missiles with nuclear charges, one of which may kill hundreds of thousands of people, will hardly have the experience of killing anybody in the sense in which a soldier had this experience when he used his bayonet or a machine gun. Yet, even though the act of launching nuclear weapons is consciously nothing more than faithful obedience of an order, there remains a question of whether or not in deeper layers of the personality there must exist, if not destructive impulses, yet a deep indifference to life, to make such acts possible.

I shall single out three phenomena which, in my opinion, form the basis for the most vicious and dangerous form of human orientation; these are love of death, malignant narcissism, and symbiotic-incestuous fixation. The three orientations, when combined, form the "syndrome of decay," that which *prompts men to destroy for the sake of destruction,* and to hate for the sake of hate. In opposition to the "syndrome of decay," I shall describe the "syndrome of growth"; this consists of love of life (as against love of death), love of man (as against narcissism), and independence (as against symbiotic-incestuous fixation). Only in a minority of people is either one of the two syndromes fully developed. But there is no denying that each man goes forward in the direction he has chosen: that of life or that of death; that of good or that of evil.

II
Different Forms of Violence

Even though the main part of this book will deal with malignant forms of destructiveness, I want to discuss first some other forms of violence. Not that I plan to deal with them exhaustively, but I believe that to deal with less pathological manifestations of violence might be helpful for the understanding of the severely pathological and malignant forms of destructiveness. The distinction between various types of violence is based on the distinction between their respective unconscious motivations; for only the understanding of the unconscious dynamics of behavior permits us to understand the behavior itself, its roots, its course, and the energy with which it is charged.[1]

The most normal and nonpathological form of violence is *playful violence*. We find it in those forms in which violence is exercised in the pursuit of displaying skill, not in the pursuit of destruction, not motivated by hate or destructiveness. Examples of this playful violence can be found in many instances: from the war games of primitive tribes to the Zen Buddhist art of sword fighting. In all such games of fighting it is not the aim to kill;

---

[1] For the various forms of aggression see the rich material in psychoanalytic studies, especially various articles in the volumes of *The Psychoanalytic Study of the Child* (New York: International Universities Press) ; see especially on the problem of human and animal aggression J. P. Scott, *Aggression* (Chicago: University of Chicago Press, 1958). Also Arnold H. Buss, *The Psychology of Aggression* (New York: John Wiley & Son, 1961); furthermore Leonard Berkowitz, *Aggression* (New York: McGraw-Hill Co., 1962).

even if the outcome is the death of the opponent it is, as it were, the opponent's fault for having "stood in the wrong spot." Naturally, if we speak of the absence of the wish to destroy in playful violence, this refers only to the ideal type of such games. In reality one would often find unconscious aggression and destructiveness hidden behind the explicit logic of the game. But even this being so, the main motivation in this type of violence is the display of skill, not destructiveness.

Of much greater practical significance than playful violence is *reactive violence*. By reactive violence I understand that violence which is employed in the defense of life, freedom, dignity, property—one's own or that of others. It is rooted in fear, and for this very reason it is probably the most frequent form of violence; the fear can be real or imagined, conscious or unconscious. This type of violence is in the service of life, not of death; its aim is preservation, not destruction. It is not entirely the outcome of irrational passions, but to some extent of rational calculation; hence it also implies a certain proportionality between end and means. It has been argued that from a higher spiritual plane killing—even in defense—is never morally right. But most of those who hold this conviction admit that violence in the defense of life is of a different nature than violence which aims at destructiveness for its own sake.

Very often the feeling of being threatened and the resulting reactive violence are not based upon reality, but on the manipulation of man's mind; political and religious leaders persuade their adherents that they are threatened by an enemy, and thus arouse the subjective response of reactive hostility. Hence the distinction between just and unjust wars, which is upheld by capitalist and Communist governments as well as by the Roman Catholic Church, is a most questionable one, since usually each side succeeds in presenting its position as a defense against attack.[2] There is hardly a case of an aggressive war which could not be

---

[2] In 1939 Hitler had to organize a fake attack on a Silesian radio station by alleged Polish soldiers (who were, in fact, SS men) in order to give his population the sensation of being attacked, and hence to justify his wanton attack against Poland as a "just war."

couched in terms of defense. The question of who claimed defense rightly is usually decided by the victors, and sometimes only much later by more objective historians. The tendency of pretending that any war is a defensive one shows two things. First of all that the majority of people, at least in most civilized countries, cannot be made to kill and to die unless they are first convinced that they are doing so in order to defend their lives and freedom; second, it shows that it is not difficult to persuade millions of people that they are in danger of being attacked, and hence that they are called upon to defend themselves. Such persuasion depends most of all on a lack of independent thinking and feeling, and on the emotional dependence of the vast majority of people on their political leaders. Provided there is this dependence, almost anything presented with force and persuasion will be accepted as real. The psychological results of the acceptance of a belief in an alleged threat are, of course, the same as those of a real threat. People *feel* threatened, and in order to defend themselves are willing to kill and to destroy. In the case of paranoid delusions of persecution we find the same mechanism, only not on a group basis, but on an individual one. In both instances, subjectively the person feels in danger and reacts aggressively.

Another aspect of reactive violence is the kind of violence which is produced by *frustration.* We find aggressive behavior in animals, children, and adults, when a wish or a need is frustrated.[3] Such aggressive behavior constitutes an attempt, although often a futile one, to attain the frustrated aim through the use of violence. It is clearly an aggression in the service of life, and not one for the sake of destruction. Since frustration of needs and desires has been an almost universal occurrence in most societies until today, there is no reason to be surprised that violence and aggression are constantly produced and exhibited.

Related to the aggression resulting from frustration is hostility engendered by *envy* and *jealousy.* Both jealousy and envy consti-

---

[3] Cf. the rich material in J. Dollard, L. W. Doob, N. E. Miller, O. H. Mowrer, and R. R. Sears. *Frustration and Aggression* (New Haven: Yale University Press, 1939).

tute a special kind of frustration. They are caused by the fact that B has an object which A desires, or is loved by a person whose love A desires. Hate and hosility is aroused in A against B who receives that which A wants, and cannot have. Envy and jealousy are frustrations, accentuated by the fact that not only does A not get what he wants, but that another person is favored instead. The story of Cain, unloved through no fault of his own, who kills the favored brother, and the story of Joseph and his brothers, are classical versions of jealousy and envy. Psychoanalytic literature offers a wealth of clinical data on these same phenomena.

Another type of violence related to reactive violence but already a step further in the direction of pathology is _revengeful violence._ In reactive violence the aim is to avert the threatened injury, for this reason such violence serves the biological function of survival. In revengeful violence, on the other hand, the injury has already been done, and hence the violence has no function of defense. It has the irrational function of undoing magically what has been done realistically. We find revengeful violence in individuals as well as among primitive and civilized groups. In analyzing the irrational nature of this type of violence we can go a step further. The revenge motive is in inverse proportion to the strength and productiveness of a group or of an individual. The impotent and the cripple have only one recourse to restore their self-esteem if it has been shattered by having been injured: to take revenge according to the _lex talionis_: "an eye for an eye." On the other hand the person who lives productively has no, or little, such need. Even if he has been hurt, insulted, and injured, the very process of living productively makes him forget the injury of the past. The ability to produce proves to be stronger than the wish for revenge. The truth of this analysis can be easily established by empirical data on the individual and on the social scale. Psychoanalytic material demonstrates that the mature, productive person is less motivated by the desire for revenge than the neurotic person who has difficulties in living independently and fully, and who is often prone to stake his whole existence on the wish for revenge. In severe psychopathology, revenge becomes the dominant aim of his life, since without revenge not only self-esteem, but the sense of self and of identity threaten to collapse. Similarly we find that in the most backward groups (in the economic or cultural and emotional aspects) the sense of revenge (for example, for a past national defeat) seems to be strongest. Thus the lower middle classes, which are those most deprived in industrialized nations, are in many countries the focus of revenge feelings, just as they are the focus of racialist and nationalist feelings. By means of a "projective questionnaire"[4] it would be easy to establish the correlation between the intensity of revenge feelings and economic and cultural impoverishment. More complicated probably is the understanding of revenge among primitive societies. Many primitive societies have intense and even institutionalized feelings and patterns of revenge, and the whole group feels obliged to avenge the injury inflicted on one of its members. It is likely that two factors play a decisive role here. The first is much the same as the one mentioned above: the atmosphere of psychic scarcity which pervades the primitive group and which makes revenge a necessary means of restitution for a loss. The second is narcissism, a phenomenon which is discussed at length in Chapter 4. Suffice it to say here that in view of the intense narcissism with which the primitive group is endowed, any insult to its self-image is so devastating that it will quite naturally arouse intense hostility.

Closely related to revengeful violence is a source of destructiveness which is due to the *shattering of faith* which often occurs in the life of a child. What is meant here by the "shattering of faith"?

A child starts life with faith in goodness, love, justice. The infant has faith in his mother's breasts, in her readiness to cover him when he is cold, to comfort him when he is sick. This faith can be faith in father, mother, in a grandparent, or in any other

---

[4] An open-ended questionnaire, the answers to which are interpreted with regard to their unconscious and unintended meaning, in order to give data not on "opinions" but on the forces working unconsciously within the individual.

person close to him; it can be expressed as faith in God. In many individuals this faith is shattered at an early age. The child hears father lying in an important matter; he sees his cowardly fright of mother, ready to betray him (the child) in order to appease her; he witnesses the parents' sexual intercourse, and may experience father as a brutal beast; he is unhappy or frightened, and neither one of the parents, who are allegedly so concerned for him, notices it, or even if he tells them, pays any attention. There are any number of times when the original faith in love, truthfulness, justice of the parents is shattered. Sometimes, in children who are brought up religiously, the loss of faith refers directly to God. A child experiences the death of a little bird he loves, or of a friend, or of a sister, and his faith in God as being good and just is shattered. But it does not make much difference whether it is faith in a person or in God which is shattered. It is always the faith in life, in the possibility of trusting it, of having confidence in it, which is broken. It is of course true that every child goes through a number of disillusionments; but what matters is the sharpness and severity of a particular disappointment. Often this first and crucial experience of shattering of faith takes place at an early age: at four, five, six, or even much earlier, at a period of life about which there is little memory. Often the final shattering of faith takes place at a much later age. Being betrayed by a friend, by a sweetheart, by a teacher, by a religious or political leader in whom one had trust. Seldom is it one single occurrence, but rather a number of small experiences which accumulatively shatter a person's faith. The reactions to such experiences vary. One person may react by losing the dependency on the particular person who has disappointed him, by becoming more independent himself and being able to find new friends, teachers, or loved ones whom he trusts and in whom he has faith. This is the most desirable reaction to early disappointments. In many other instances the outcome is that the person remains skeptical, hopes for a miracle that will restore his faith, tests people, and when disappointed in turn by them tests still others or throws himself into the arms of a powerful authority (the Church, or a political party, or a leader) to regain his faith. Often he overcomes his despair at having lost faith in life by a frantic pursuit of worldly aims—money, power, or prestige.

The reaction which is important in the context of violence is still another one. The deeply deceived and disappointed person can also begin to hate life. If there is nothing and nobody to believe in, if one's faith in goodness and justice has all been a foolish illusion, if life is ruled by the Devil rather than by God—then, indeed, life becomes hateful; one can no longer bear the pain of disappointment. One wishes to prove that life is evil, that men are evil, that oneself is evil. The disappointed believer and lover of life thus will be turned into a cynic and a destroyer. This destructiveness is one of despair; disappointment in life has led to hate of life.

In my clinical experience these deep-seated experiences of loss of faith are frequent, and often constitute the most significant *leitmotiv* in the life of a person. The same holds true in social life, where leaders in whom one trusted prove to be evil or incompetent. If the reaction is not one of greater independence, it is often one of cynicism or destructiveness.

While all these forms of violence are still in the service of life realistically, magically, or at least as the result of damage to or disappointment in life, the next form to be discussed, *compensatory violence*, is a more pathological form, even though less drastically so than necrophilia, which is discussed in Chapter 3.

By compensatory violence I understand violence as a *substitute* for productive activity occurring in an impotent person. In order to understand the term "impotence" as it is used here, we must review some preliminary considerations. While man is the object of natural and social forces which rule him, he is at the same time not *only* the object of circumstances. He has the will, the capacity, and the freedom to transform and to change the world—within certain limits. What matters here is not the scope of will and freedom,[5] but the fact that man cannot tolerate absolute passivity. He is driven to make his imprint on the world, to transform and to change, and not only *to be* trans-

---

[5] The problem of freedom is dealt with in Chapter 6.

formed and changed. This human need is expressed in the early cave drawings, in all the arts, in work, and in sexuality. All these activities are the result of man's capacity to direct his will toward a goal and to sustain his effort until the goal is reached. The capacity to thus use his powers is *potency*. (Sexual potency is only one of the forms of potency.) If, for reasons of weakness, anxiety, incompetence, etc., man is not able to *act*, if he is impotent, he suffers; this suffering due to impotence is rooted in the very fact that the human equilibrium has been disturbed, that man cannot accept the state of complete powerlessness without attempting to restore his capacity to act. But can he, and how? One way is to submit to and identify with a person or group having power. By this symbolic participation in another person's life, man has the illusion of acting, when in reality he only submits to and becomes a part of those who act. The other way, and this is the one which interests us most in this context, is man's power to destroy.

To create life is to transcend one's status as a creature that is thrown into life as dice are thrown out of a cup. But to destroy life also means to transcend it and to escape the unbearable suffering of complete passivity. To create life requires certain qualities which the impotent person lacks. To destroy life requires only one quality—the use of force. The impotent man, if he has a pistol, a knife, or a strong arm, can transcend life by destroying it in others or in himself. He thus *takes revenge on life for negating itself to him.* Compensatory violence is precisely that violence which has its roots in and which compensates for impotence. The man who cannot create wants to destroy. In creating and in destroying he transcends his role as a mere creature. Camus expressed this idea succinctly when he had Caligula say: "I live, I kill, I exercise the rapturous power of a destroyer, compared with which the power of a creator is merest child's play." This is the violence of the cripple, of those to whom life has denied the capacity for any positive expression of their specifically human powers. They need to destroy precisely because they are human, since being human means transcending thing-ness.

Closely related to compensatory violence is the drive for complete and absolute control over a living being, animal or man. This drive is the essence of *sadism*. In sadism, as I have pointed out in *Escape from Freedom*,[6] the wish to inflict pain on others is not the essence. All the different forms of sadism which we can observe go back to one essential impulse, namely, to have complete mastery over another person, to make of him a helpless object of our will, to become his god, to do with him as one pleases. To humiliate him, to enslave him, are means toward this end, and the most radical aim is to make him suffer, since there is no greater power over another person than that of forcing him to undergo suffering without his being able to defend himself. The pleasure in complete domination over another person (or other animate creature) is the very essence of the sadistic drive. Another way of formulating the same thought is to say that the aim of sadism is to transform a man into a thing, something animate into something inanimate, since by complete and absolute control the living loses one essential quality of life—freedom.

Only if one has fully experienced the intensity and frequency of destructive and sadistic violence in individuals and in masses can one understand that compensatory violence is not something superficial, the result of evil influences, bad habits, and so on. It is a power in man as intense and strong as his wish to live. It is so strong precisely because it constitutes the revolt of life against its being crippled; man has a potential for destructive and sadistic violence because he is human, because he is not a thing, and because he must try to destroy life if he cannot create it. The Colosseum in Rome, in which thousands of impotent people got their greatest pleasure by seeing men devoured by beasts, or killing each other, is the great monument to sadism.

From these considerations follows something else. Compensatory violence is the result of unlived and crippled life, and its necessary result. It can be suppressed by fear of punishment, it can even be deflected by spectacles and amusements of all kinds. Yet it remains as a potential in its full strength, and whenever

[6] New York: Holt, Rinehart and Winston, 1941.

the suppressing forces weaken, it becomes manifest. The only cure for compensatory destructiveness is the development of the creative potential in man, his capacity to make productive use of his human powers. Only if man ceases to be crippled will he cease to be a destroyer and a sadist, and only conditions in which man can be interested in life can do away with those impulses which make the past and present history of man so shameful. Compensatory violence is not, like reactive violence, in the service of life; it is the pathological *substitute* for life; it indicates the crippling and emptiness of life. But in its very negation of life it still demonstrates man's need to be alive and not to be a cripple.

There is one last type of violence which needs to be described: *archaic "blood thirst."* This is not the violence of the cripple; it is the blood thirst of the man who is still completely enveloped in his tie to nature. His is a passion for killing as a way to transcend life, inasmuch as he is afraid of moving forward and of being fully human (a choice I shall discuss later). In the man who seeks an answer to life by regressing to the pre-individual state of existence, by becoming like an animal and thus being freed from the burden of reason, *blood* becomes the essence of life; to shed blood is to feel alive, to be strong, to be unique, to be above all others. Killing becomes the great intoxication, the great self-affirmation on the most archaic level. Conversely, to be killed is the only logical alternative to killing. This is the balance of life in the archaic sense: to kill as many as one can, and when one's life is thus satiated with blood, one is ready to be killed. Killing in this sense is not essentially love of death. It is affirmation and transcendence of life on the level of deepest regression. We can observe this thirst for blood in individuals; sometimes in their fantasies or dreams, sometimes in severe mental sickness or in murder. We can oberve it in a minority in times of war—international or civil—when the normal social inhibitions have been removed. We observe it in archaic society, in which killing (or being killed) is the polarity which governs life. We can observe this in phenomena like the human sacrifices of the Aztecs, in the blood revenge practiced in places like

Monteneego[7] or Corsica in the role of blood as a sacrifice to God
in the Old Testament. One of the most lucid descriptions of
this joy of killing is to be found in G. Flaubert's short story
The Legend of St. Julian the Hospitaler.[8] Flaubert describes
a man about whom it is prophesied at birth that he will become
a great conqueror and a great saint; he grew up as a normal child
until one day he discovered the excitement of killing. At the
church services he had observed several times a little mouse
scurrying from a hole in the wall; it angered him; he was
determined to rid himself of it. "So, having closed the door
and having sprinkled some cake crumbs on the altar steps,
he posted himself in front of the hole, with a stick in his hand.
After a very long time a small pink nose appeared, then the
whole mouse. He struck a slight blow, and stood aghast over
this tiny body which no longer moved. A drop of blood stained
the flagstone. He wiped it away quickly with his sleeve, threw
the mouse outside and said nothing to anyone." Later, when
strangling a bird, "the bird's writhing made his heart thump,
filling him with a savage, tumultuous delight." Having experienced the exaltation of shedding blood, he became obsessed with
killing animals. No animal was too strong or too swift to escape
being killed by him. Shedding blood became the utmost affirmation of himself as the one way to transcend all life. For years
his only passion and only excitement was killing animals. He
returned at night "covered with blood and mud, and reeking
with the odor of wild beasts. He became like them." He almost
attained the aim of being transformed into an animal, yet being
human he could not attain it. A voice told him that he would
eventually kill his father and mother. Frightened he fled his castle,
stopped killing animals, and instead became a feared and famous
leader of troops. As a reward for one of his greatest victories he
was given the hand of an extraordinarily beautiful and loving
woman. He stopped being a warrior, settles down with her to
what could be a life of bliss—yet he is bored and depressed.

[7] Cf. the picture given by Djilas of the Montenegrin way of life in which
he describes killing as the greatest pride and intoxication a man can experience.
[8] New York: New American Library, 1964.

One day he began hunting again, but a strange force made his shots impotent. "Then all the animals that he had hunted reappeared and formed a tight circle around him. Some sat on their haunches, others stood erect. Julian, in their midst, was frozen with terror, incapable of the slightest movement." He decided to return to his wife and to his castle; in the meantime his old parents had arrived there and had been given by his wife her own bed; mistaking them for his wife and a lover, he slew them both. When he had attained the depth of regression, the great turn came. He became, indeed, a saint, devoting his life to the poor and the sick, and eventually embracing a leper to give him warmth, "Julian ascended toward the blue expanses, face to face with our Lord Jesus, who bore him to heaven."

Flaubert describes in this story the essence of blood thirst. It is the intoxication with life in its most archaic form; hence a person, after having reached this most archaic level of relatedness to life, can return to the highest level of development, to that of the affirmation of life by his humanity. It is important to see that this thirst for killing, as I observed earlier, is not the same as the love of death, which is described in Chapter 3. Blood is experienced as the essence of life; to shed the blood of another is to fertilize mother earth with what she needs to be fertile. (Compare the Aztec belief in the necessity to shed blood as a condition for the continued functioning of the cosmos, or the story of Cain and Abel.) Even if one's own blood is shed, one fertilizes the earth, and becomes one with her.

It seems that at this level of regression blood is the equivalent of semen; earth is the equivalent of mother-woman. Semen-egg are the expressions of the male-female polarity, a polarity which becomes central only when man has begun to emerge fully from earth, to the point that woman becomes the object of his desire and love.[9] The shedding of blood ends in death; the shedding of semen in birth. But the goal of the first is, like that of the second, the affirmation of life, even though hardly above the level of animal existence. The killer can become the lover if he

[9] When the biblical story tells us that God made Eve to be a "helpmate" to Adam this new function is indicated.

becomes fully born, if he casts away his tie to earth, and if he overcomes his narcissism. Yet it cannot be denied that if he is unable to do this, his narcissism and his archaic fixation will entrap him in a way of life which is so close to the way of death that the difference between the bloodthirsty man and the lover of death may become hard to distinguish.

III
Love of Death and Love of Life

In the previous chapter we discussed forms of violence and aggression which can still be considered more or less benign, inasmuch as they serve (or seem to serve) either directly or indirectly the purposes of life. In this chapter and the following ones we shall deal with tendencies which are directed *against* life, which form the nucleus of severe mental sickness, and which can be said to be the essence of true evil. We shall deal with three different kinds of orientation: necrophilia (biophilia), narcissism, and symbiotic fixation to mother.

I shall show that all three have benign forms which can even be so minimal in weight that they may not be considered pathological at all. Our main emphasis, however, will be on the malignant forms of all three orientations, which in their gravest forms converge and eventually form "the syndrome of decay"; this syndrome represents the quintessence of evil; it is at the same time the most severe pathology and the root of the most vicious destructiveness and inhumanity.

I do not know of a better introduction to the heart of the problem of necrophilia than a short statement made by the Spanish philosopher Unamuno in 1936. The occasion was a speech by General Millán Astray at the University of Salamanca, whose rector Unamuno was at the time of the beginning of the Spanish Civil War. The general's favorite motto was "Viva la muerte!" (Long live death!), and one of his followers shouted it from the back of the hall. When the general had finished his speech Unamuno rose and said:

". . . Just now I heard a necrophilous and senseless cry: "Long live death!" And I, who have spent my life shaping paradoxes which have aroused the uncomprehending anger of others, I must tell you, as an expert authority, that this outlandish paradox is repellent to me. General Millán Astray is a cripple. Let it be said without any slighting undertone. He is a war invalid. So was Cervantes. Unfortunately there are too many cripples in Spain just now. And soon there will be even more of them if God does not come to our aid. It pains me to think that General Millán Astray should dictate the pattern of mass psychology. A cripple who lacks the spiritual greatness of a Cervantes is wont to seek ominous relief in causing mutilation around him." At this Millán Astray was unable to restrain himself any longer. "Abajo la inteligencia!" (Down with intelligence!) he shouted. "Long live death!" There was a clamor of support for this remark from the Falangists. But Unamuno went on: "This is the temple of the intellect. And I am its high priest. It is you who profane its sacred precincts. You will win, because you have more than enough brute force. But you will not convince. For to convince you need to persuade. And in order to persuade you would need what you lack: Reason and Right in the struggle. I consider it futile to exhort you to think of Spain. I have done."[1]

Unamuno, in speaking of the necrophilous character of the cry "Long live death," touched upon the core of the problem of evil. There is no more fundamental distinction between men, psychologically and morally, than the one between those who love death and those who love life, between the *necrophilous* and the *biophilous*. This is not meant to convey that a person is necessarily either entirely necrophilous or entirely biophilous. There are some who are totally devoted to death, and these are insane. There are others who are entirely devoted to life, and these strike us as having accomplished the highest aim of which man is capable. In many, both the biophilous and the necrophilous trends are present, but in various blends. What matters here, as always in living phenomena, is which trend is the stronger,

[1] Quoted from H. Thomas, *The Spanish Civil War* (New York: Harper & Row, 1961), pp. 354-55. Thomas quotes Unamuno's speech from L. Portillo's translation of this speech, published in *Horizon* and reprinted in Connolly, *The Golden Horizon*, pp. 397-409. Unamuno remained under house arrest until his death a few months later.

so that it determines man's behavior—not the complete absence or presence of one of the two orientations.

Literally, "necrophilia" means "love of the dead" (as "biophilia" means "love of life"). The term is customarily used to denote a sexual perversion, namely the desire to possess the dead body (of a woman) for purposes of sexual intercourse,[2] or a morbid desire to be in the presence of a dead body. But, as is often the case, a sexual perversion presents only the more overt and clear picture of an orientation which is to be found without sexual admixture in many people. Unamuno saw this clearly when he applied the word "necrophilous" to the General's speech. He did not imply that the General was obsessed with a sexual perversion, but that he hated life and loved death.

Strangely enough, necrophilia as a general orientation has never been described in the psychoanalytic literature, although it is related to Freud's *anal-sadistic character* as well as to his *death instinct*. While I shall try to discuss these connections later, I will now proceed to give a description of the necrophilous person.

The person with the necrophilous orientation is one who is attracted to and fascinated by all that is not alive, all that is dead; corpses, decay, feces, dirt. Necrophiles are those people who love to talk about sickness, about burials, about death. They come to life precisely when they can talk about death. A clear example of the pure necrophilous type is Hitler. He was fascinated by destruction, and the smell of death was sweet to him. While in the years of his success it may have appeared that he wanted to destroy only those whom he considered his enemies, the days of the *Götterdämmerung* at the end showed that his deepest satisfaction lay in witnessing total and absolute *destruction:* that of the German people, of those around him, and of himself. A report from the First World War, while not proved, makes good sense: a soldier saw Hitler standing in a trancelike mood, gazing at a decayed corpse and unwilling to move away.

The necrophilous dwell in the past, never in the future. Their

[2] Krafft-Ebing, Hirschfeld, and others have given many examples of patients obsessed with this desire.

feelings are essentially sentimental, that is, they nurse the memory of feelings which they had yesterday—or believe that they had. They are cold, distant, devotees of "law and order." Their values are precisely the reverse of the values we connect with normal life: not life, but death excites and satisfies them.

Characteristic for the necrophile is his attitude toward force. Force is, to quote Simone Weil's definition, the capacity to transform a man into a corpse. Just as sexuality can create life, force can destroy it. All force is, in the last analysis, based on the power to kill. I may not kill a person but only deprive him of his freedom; I may want only to humiliate him or to take away his possessions—but whatever I do, behind all these actions stands my capacity to kill and my willingness to kill. The lover of death necessarily loves force. For him the greatest achievement of man is not to give life, but to destroy it; the use of force is not a transitory action forced upon him by circumstances—it is a way of life.

This explains why the necrophile is truly enamored of force. Just as for the lover of life the fundamental polarity in man is that between male and female, for the necrophile there exists another and very different polarity: that between those who have the power to kill and those who lack this power. For him there are only two "sexes": the powerful and the powerless; the killers and the killed. He is in love with the killers and despises those who are killed. Not rarely this "being in love with the killers" is to be taken literally; they are his objects of sexual attraction and fantasies, only less drastically so than in the perversion mentioned above or in the perversion of necrophagia (the desire to eat a corpse) a desire which can be found not rarely in the dreams of necrophilous persons. I know of a number of dreams of necrophilous persons in which they have sexual intercourse with an old woman or man by whom they are in no way physically attracted, but whom they fear and admire for their power and destructiveness.

The influence of men like Hitler or Stalin lies precisely in their unlimited capacity and willingness to kill. For this they were loved by the necrophiles. Of the rest, many were afraid of them, and preferred to admire, rather than to be aware of their fear; many others did not sense the necrophilous quality of these leaders, and saw in them the builders, saviors, good fathers. If the necrophilous leaders had not pretended that they were build-ers and protectors, the number of people attracted to them would hardly have been sufficient to help them to seize power, and the number of those repelled by them would probably soon have led to their downfall.

While life is characterized by growth in a structured, func-tional manner, the necrophilous person loves all that does not grow, all that is mechanical. The necrophilous person is driven by the desire to transform the organic into the inorganic, to ap-proach life mechanically, as if all living persons were things. All living processes, feelings, and thoughts are transformed into things. Memory, rather than experience; having, rather than being, is what counts. The necrophilous person can relate to an object—a flower or a person—only if he possesses it; hence a threat to his possession is a threat to himself; if he loses posses-sion he loses contact with the world. That is why we find the paradoxical reaction that he would rather lose life than posses-sion, even though by losing life he who possesses has ceased to exist. He loves control, and in the act of controlling he kills life. He is deeply afraid of life, because it is disorderly and uncon-trollable by its very nature. The woman who wrongly claims to be the mother of the child in the story of Solomon's judgment is typical for this tendency; she would rather have a properly divided dead child than lose a living one. To the necrophilous person justice means correct division, and they are willing to kill or die for the sake of what they call justice. "Law and order" for them are idols—everything that threatens law and order is felt as a satanic attack against their supreme values.

The necrophilous person is attracted to darkness and night. In mythology and poetry he is attracted to caves, or to the depth of the ocean, or depicted as being blind. (The trolls in Ibsen's *Peer Gynt* are a good example; they are blind,[3] they live in caves,

[3] This symbolic meaning of blindness is quite different from that where it means "true insight."

their only value is the narcissistic one of something "home brewed" or home made.) All that is away from or directed against life attracts him. He wants to return to the darkness of the womb, and to the past of inorganic or animal existence. He is essentially oriented to the past, not to the future which he hates and is afraid of. Related to this is his craving for certainty. But life is never certain, never predictable, never controllable; in order to make life controllable it must be transformed into death; death, indeed, is the only certainty in life.

The necrophilous tendencies are usually most clearly exhibited in a person's dreams. These deal with murder, blood, corpses, skulls, feces; sometimes also with men transformed into machines or acting like machines. An occasional dream of this type may occur in many people without indicating necrophilia. In the necrophilous person dreams of this type are frequent and sometimes repetitive.

The highly necrophilous person can often be recognized by his appearance and his gestures. He is cold, his skin looks dead, and often he has an expression on his face as though he were smelling a bad odor. (This expression could be clearly seen in Hitler's face.) He is orderly, obsessive, pedantic. This aspect of the necrophilous person has been demonstrated to the world in the figure of Eichmann. Eichmann was fascinated by bureaucratic order and death. His supreme values were obedience and the proper functioning of the organization. He transported Jews as he would have transported coal. That they were human beings was hardly within the field of his vision, hence even the problem of whether he hated or did not hate his victims is irrelevant.

But examples of the necrophilous character are by no means to be found only among the inquisitors, the Hitlers, and the Eichmanns. There are any number of individuals who do not have the opportunity and the power to kill, yet whose necrophilia expresses itself in other and, superficially seen, more harmless ways. An example is the mother who will always be interested in her child's sicknesses, in his failures, in dark prognoses for the future; at the same time she will not be impressed by a favorable change; she will not respond to the child's joy; she will not notice anything new that is growing within him. We might find that her dreams deal with sickness, death, corpses, blood. She does not harm the child in any obvious way, yet she may slowly strangle his joy of life, his faith in growth, and eventually she will infect him with her own necrophilous orientation.

Many times the necrophilous orientation is in conflict with opposite tendencies, so that a peculiar balance is achieved. An outstanding example of this type of necrophilous character was C. G. Jung. In his posthumously published autobiography[4] he gives ample evidence for this. His dreams are mostly filled with corpses, blood, killings. As a typical manifestation of his necrophilous orientation in real life, I will mention the following: While Jung's house in Bollingen was being built, the corpse of a French soldier was found who had been drowned 150 years earlier at the time when Napoleon invaded Switzerland. Jung took a picture of the corpse and hung it on his wall. He buried him and fired three shots over his grave as a military salute. On the surface this action may appear slightly odd but otherwise as not having any significance. Yet it is one of those many "insignificant" actions which express an underlying orientation more clearly than the intentional, important acts do. Freud himself noticed Jung's death orientation many years earlier. When he and Jung were embarking for the United States, Jung spoke a great deal about the well-preserved corpses which had been found in the marshes near Hamburg. Freud disliked this kind of talk, and told Jung that he spoke so much of the corpses because unconsciously he was filled with death wishes against him (Freud). Jung denied this indignantly, yet some years later, around the time of his separation from Freud, he had the following dream. He felt that he (together with a black native) had to kill *Siegfried*. He went out with a rifle, and when Siegfried appeared on the crest of a mountain he killed him. He then felt horror-stricken and frightened that his crime might be discovered. But fortunately a heavy rain fell which washed away all traces of the crime.

[4] C. G. Jung, *Memories, Dreams, Reflections*, ed. by Aniéla Jaffé, New York: Pantheon Books, 1963. Cf. my discussion of this book in the *Scientific American* of September, 1963.

Jung woke up thinking that he must kill himself unless he could understand the dream. After some thought he came to the following "understanding": killing Siegfried means killing the hero within himself, and thus expressing his own humility. The slight change from *Sigmund* to *Siegfried* was enough to enable a man whose greatest skill was the interpretation of dreams, to hide the real meaning of this dream from himself. If one asks oneself the question how such intense repression is possible, the answer is that the dream was a manifestation of his necrophilous orientation, and since this entire orientation was intensely repressed, Jung could not afford to be aware of the meaning of this dream. It fits into the picture that Jung was fascinated by the past, and rarely by the present and the future; that stones were his favorite material, and that as a child he had a fantasy about God dropping a big turd on a church and thus destroying it. His sympathies for Hitler and his racial theories are another expression of his affinity with death-loving people.

However, Jung was an unusually creative person, and creation is the very opposite of necrophilia. He solved the conflict within himself by balancing his destructive powers against his wish and ability to cure, and by making his interest in the past, in death and destruction, the subject matter of his brilliant speculations.

In this description of the necrophilous orientation I may have given the impression that *all* the features described here are necessarily found in the necrophilous person. It is true that such divergent features as the wish to kill, the worship of force, the attraction to death and dirt, sadism, the wish to transform the organic into the inorganic through "order," are all part of the same basic orientation. Yet as far as individuals are concerned, there are considerable differences with regard to the strength of these respective trends. Any one of the features mentioned here may be more pronounced in one person than in another; furthermore, the degree to which a person is necrophilous in comparison with his biophilous aspects, and finally the degree to which a person is aware of the necrophilous tendencies or rationalizes them, varies considerably from person to person. Yet the concept of the necrophilous type is by no means an abstraction or a summary of various disparate behavior trends. Necrophilia constitutes a fundamental orientation; it is the one answer to life which is in complete opposition to life; it is the most morbid and the most dangerous among the orientations to life of which man is capable. It is the true perversion: while being alive, not life but death is loved; not growth but destruction. The necrophilous person, if he dares to be aware of what he feels, expresses the motto of his life when he says, "Long live death!"

The opposite of the necrophilous orientation is the *biophilous;* its essence is love of life in contrast to love of death. Like necrophilia, biophilia is not constituted by a single trait, but represents a total orientation, an entire way of being. It is manifested in a person's bodily processes, in his emotions, in his thoughts, in his gestures; the biophilous orientation expresses itself in the whole man. The most elementary form of this orientation is expressed in the tendency of all living organisms to live. In contrast to Freud's assumption concerning the "death instinct," I agree with the assumption made by many biologists and philosophers that it is an inherent quality of all living substance to live, to preserve its existence; as Spinoza expressed it: "Everything insofar as it is itself, endeavors to persist in its own being."[5] He called this endeavor the very essence of the thing in question.[6]

We observe this tendency to live in all living substance around us; in the grass that breaks through the stones to get light and to live; in the animal that will fight to the last in order to escape death; in man who will do almost anything to preserve his life.

The tendency to preserve life and to fight against death is the most elementary form of the biophilous orientation, and is common to all living substance. Inasmuch as it is a tendency to *preserve* life, and to *fight* death, it represents only *one* aspect of the drive toward life. The other aspect is a more positive one: living substance has the tendency to integrate and to unite; it

[5] *Ethic,* III, Prop. VI.
[6] *Ibid.,* Prop. VII.

tends to fuse with different and opposite entities, and to grow in a structural way. Unification and integrated growth are characteristic of all life processes, not only as far as cells are concerned, but also with regard to feeling and thinking.

The most elementary expression of this tendency is the fusion between cells and organisms, from nonsexual cell fusion to sexual union among animals and man. In the latter, sexual union is based on the attraction between the male and the females poles. The male-female polarity constitutes the core of that need for fusion on which the life of the human species depends. It seems that for this very reason nature has provided man with the most intense pleasure in the fusion of the two poles. Biologically, the result of this fusion is normally the creation of a new being. The cycle of life is that of union, birth, and growth—just as the cycle of death is that of cessation of growth, disintegration, decay.

However, even the sexual instinct, while *biologically* serving life, is not necessarily one which *psychologically* expresses biophilia. It seems that there is hardly any intense emotion which cannot be attracted to and blended with the sexual instinct. Vanity, the desire for wealth, for adventure, and even the attraction to death can, as it were, commission the sexual instinct into their service. Why this should be so is a matter for speculation. One is tempted to think that it is the cunning of nature to make the sexual instinct so pliable that it will be mobilized by any kind of intense desire, even by those which are in contradiction to life. But whatever the reason, the fact of the blending between sexual desire and destructiveness can hardly be doubted. (Freud pointed to this mixture, especially in his discussion of the blending of the death instinct with the life instinct, as occurring in sadism and masochism.) Sadism, masochism, necrophagia and coprophagia are perversions, not because they deviate from the customary standards of sexual behavior, but precisely because they signify the one fundamental perversion: the blending between life and death.[7]

The full unfolding of biophilia is to be found in the pro-

[7] Many rituals which deal with the separation of the clean (life) from the unclean (death) emphasize the importance of avoiding this perversion.

ductive orientation.[8] The person who fully loves life is attracted by the process of life and growth in all spheres. He prefers to construct rather than to retain. He is capable of wondering, and he prefers to see something new to the security of finding confirmation of the old. He loves the adventure of living more than he does certainty. His approach to life is functional rather than mechanical. He sees the whole rather than only the parts, structures rather than summations. He wants to mold and to influence by love, reason, by his example; not by force, by cutting things apart, by the bureaucratic manner of administering people as if they were things. He enjoys life and all its manifestations rather than mere excitement.

Biophilic ethics have their own principle of good and evil. Good is all that serves life; evil is all that serves death. Good is reverence for life,[9] all that enhances life, growth, unfolding. Evil is all that stifles life, narrows it down, cuts it into pieces. Joy is virtuous and sadness is sinful. Thus it is from the standpoint of biophilic ethics that the Bible mentions as the central sin of the Hebrews: "Because thou didst not serve thy Lord with joy and gladness of heart in the abundance of all things" (Deut. 28:47). The conscience of the biophilous person is not one of forcing oneself to refrain from evil and to do good. It is not the superego described by Freud, which is a strict taskmaster, employing sadism against oneself for the sake of virtue. The biophilous conscience is motivated by its attraction to life and joy; the moral effort consists in strengthening the life-loving side in oneself. For this reason the biophile does not dwell in remorse and guilt which are, after all, only aspects of self-loathing and sadness. He turns quickly to life and attempts to do good. Spinoza's *Ethic* is a striking example of biophilic morality. "Pleasure", he says, "in itself is not bad but good; contrariwise, pain in itself is bad."[10] And in the same spirit: "A free man thinks of death least of all things; and his wisdom is a medita-

[8] Cf. the discussion of the productive orientation in E. Fromm, *Man For Himself* (New York: Holt, Rinehart and Winston, 1947).

[9] This is the main thesis of Albert Schweitzer, one of the great representatives of the love of life—both in his writings and in his person.

[10] *Ethic*, IV, Prop. XLI.

tion not of death but of life."[11] Love of life underlies the various versions of humanistic philosophy. In various conceptual forms these philosophies are in the same vein as Spinoza's; they express the principle that the sane man loves life, that sadness is sin and joy is virtue, that man's aim in life is to be attracted by all that is alive and to separate himself from all that is dead and mechanical.

I have tried to give a picture of the necrophilic and the biophilic orientations in their pure forms. These pure forms are, of course, rare. The pure necrophile is insane; the pure biophile is saintly. Most people are a particular blend of the necrophilous and the biophilous orientations, and what matters is which of the two trends is dominant. Those in whom the necrophilous orientation gains dominance will slowly kill the biophilic side in themselves; usually they are not aware of their death-loving orientation; they will harden their hearts; they will act in such a way that their love of death seems to be the logical and rational response to what they experience. On the other hand, those in whom love for life still dominates, will be shocked when they discover how close they are to the "valley of the shadow of death," and this shock might awaken them to life. Hence it is very important to understand not only how strong the necrophilic tendency is in a person, but also how aware he is of it. If he believes that he dwells in the land of life when in reality he lives in the land of death, he is lost to life since he has no chance to return.

The description of the necrophilous and biophilous orientation raises the question how these concepts are related to Freud's concept of the life instinct (Eros) and the death instinct. The similarity is easy to see. Freud, when he tentatively suggested the existence of the duality of these two drives within man was deeply impressed, especially under the influence of the First World War, by the force of the destructive impulses. He revised his older theory in which the sexual instinct had been opposed to the ego instincts (both serving survival, and thus the purposes of life) for the sake of the hypothesis that both the striving for

[11] *Ibid.*, Prop. LXVII.

life and the striving for death are inherent in the very substance of life. In *Beyond the Pleasure Principle* (1920), Freud expressed the view that there was a phylogenetically older principle which he called the "repetition compulsion." The latter operates to restore a previous condition and ultimately to take organic life back to the original state of inorganic existence. "If it is true," said Freud, "that once in an inconceivably remote past, and in an unimaginable way, life rose out of inanimate matter, then, in accordance with our hypothesis, an instinct must have at that time come into being, whose aim it was to abolish life once more and to re-establish the inorganic state of things. If in this instinct we recognize the impulse to self-destruction in our hypotheses, then we can regard that impulse as the manifestation of a *death* instinct which can never be absent in any vital process."[12]

The death instinct may be actually observed either turned outward against others, or inward against ourselves, and often blended with the sexual instinct, as in sadistic and masochistic perversions. Opposite to the death instinct is the life instinct. While the death instinct (sometimes called Thanatos in the psychoanalytic literature, although not by Freud himself) has the function of separating and disintegrating, Eros has the function of binding, integrating, and uniting organisms to each other and cells within the organism. Each individual's life, then, is a battlefield for these two fundamental instincts: "the effort of Eros to combine organic substances into ever larger unities" and the efforts of the death instinct which tends to undo precisely what Eros is trying to accomplish.

Freud himself proposed the new theory only hesitantly and tentatively. This is not surprising, since it was based on the hypothesis of the repetition compulsion which in itself was at best an unproved speculation. In fact, none of the arguments in favor of his dualistic theory seem to answer objections based on many contradictory data. Most living beings seem to fight for life with an extraordinary tenacity, and only exceptionally do they tend to destroy themselves. Furthermore, destructiveness varies

[12] S. Freud, *New Introductory Lectures On Psycho-Analysis* (New York: W. W. Norton Co., 1933).

enormously among individuals, and by no means in such a way that the variation is only one between the respective outward- and inward-directed manifestations of the death instinct. We see some persons who are characterized by an especially intense passion to destroy others, while the majority do not show this degree of destructiveness. This lesser degree of destructiveness against others is, however, not matched by a correspondingly higher degree of self-destruction, masochism, illness, etc.[13] Considering all these objections to Freud's theories, it is not surprising that a large number of otherwise orthodox analysts, like O. Fenichel, refused to accept his theory of the death instinct, or accepted it only conditionally and with great qualifications.

I suggest a development of Freud's theory in the following direction: The contradiction between Eros and destruction, between the affinity to life and the affinity to death is, indeed, the most fundamental contradiction which exists in man. This duality, however, is not one of two biologically inherent instincts, relatively constant and always battling with each other until the final victory of the death instinct, but it is one between the primary and most fundamental tendency of life—to persevere in life[14]—and its contradiction, which comes into being when man fails in this goal. In this view the "death instinct" is a *malignant* phenomenon which grows and takes over to the extent to which Eros does not unfold. The death instinct represents *psychopathology* and not, as in Freud's view, a part of *normal biology*. The life instinct thus constitutes the primary potentiality in man; the death instinct a secondary potentiality.[15] The primary potentiality develops if the appropriate conditions for life are present, just as a seed grows only if the proper conditions of

[13] Cf. the discussion of statistics on suicide and homicide in E. Fromm, *The Sane Society* (New York: Holt, Rinehart and Winston, 1955), Chap. 1.

[14] Freud takes care of the objection that if the death instinct is so strong people would normally tend to commit suicide by saying that "the organism wishes to die in its own fashion. Hence arises the paradoxical situation that the living organism struggles most energetically against events (dangers, in fact) which might help it to attain its life's goal rapidly—by a kind of short circuit" (*Beyond the Pleasure Principle*, p. 51).

[15] Cf. my analysis of destructiveness and the distinction between primary and secondary potentialities in *Man for Himself*, Chap. 5, sec. A.

moisture, temperature, etc., are given. If the proper conditions are not present, the necrophilous tendencies will emerge and dominate the person.

Which are the conditions that are responsible for necrophilia? From the standpoint of Freud's theory one must expect that the strength of the life and death instincts (respectively) remains constant, and that for the death instinct there is only the alternative of its being turned either outward or inward. Hence environmental factors can account only for the direction which the death instinct takes, not for its intensity. If, on the other hand, one follows the hypothesis presented here, one must ask this question: Which factors make for the development of the necrophilous and the biophilous orientations in general; and more specifically, for the greater or lesser intensity of the death-loving orientation in a given individual or group?

To this important question I do not have a full answer. Further study of this problem is, in my opinion, of the utmost importance. Nevertheless I can venture some tentative answers which I have arrived at on the basis of my clinical experience in psychoanalysis and on the basis of observation and analysis of group behavior.

The most important condition for the development of the love of life in the child is for him to be with people who love life. Love of life is just as contagious as love of death. It communicates itself without words, explanations, and certainly without any preaching that one ought to love life. It is expressed in gestures more than in ideas, in the tone of voice more than in words. It can be observed in the whole atmosphere of a person or group, rather than in the explicit principles and rules according to which they organize their lives. Among the specific conditions necessary for the development of biophilia I shall mention the following: warm, affectionate contact with others during infancy; freedom, and absence of threats; teaching—by example rather than by preaching—of the principles conducive to inner harmony and strength; guidance in the "art of living"; stimulating influence of and response to others; a way of life that is genuinely interesting. The very opposite of these conditions furthers the development of necrophilia: growing up among death-loving people; lack of stimulation; fright, conditions which make life routinized and uninteresting; mechanical order instead of one determined by direct and human relations among people.

As to the *social* conditions for the development of biophilia, it is evident that they are the very conditions which promote the trends I have just mentioned with regard to individual development. It is possible, however, to speculate further about the social conditions, even though the following remarks are only a beginning rather than an end of such speculation.

Perhaps the most obvious factor that should be mentioned here is that of a situation of *abundance* versus *scarcity,* both economically and psychologically. As long as most of man's energy is taken up by the defense of his life against attacks, or to ward off starvation, love of life must be stunted, and necrophilia fostered. Another important social condition for the development of biophilia lies in the abolition of *injustice.* By this I do not refer here to the hoarding concept according to which it is considered injustice if everybody does not have exactly the same; I refer to a social situation in which one social class exploits another, and imposes conditions on it which do not permit the unfolding of a rich and dignified life; or in other words, where one social class is not permitted to share with others in the same basic experience of living; in the last analysis, by injustice I refer to a social situation in which a man is not an end in himself, but becomes a means for the ends of another man.

Finally, a significant condition for the development of biophilia is *freedom.* But "freedom from" political shackles is not a sufficient condition. If love for life is to develop, there must be freedom "to"; freedom to create and to construct, to wonder and to venture. Such freedom requires that the individual be active and responsible, not a slave or a well-fed cog in the machine.

Summing up, love for life will develop most in a society where there is: *security* in the sense that the basic material conditions for a dignified life are not threatened, *justice* in the sense that nobody can be an end for the purposes of another, and *freedom* in the sense that each man has the possibility to be an active and responsible member of society. The last point is of particular importance. Even a society in which security and justice are present might not be conducive to love of life if the creative self-activity of the individual is not furthered. It is not enough that men are not slaves; if social conditions further the existence of automatons, the result will not be love of life, but love of death. More about this last point will be said in the pages dealing with the problem of necrophilia in the nuclear age, specifically in relation to the problem of a bureaucratic organization of society.

I have tried to show that the concepts of biophilia and necrophilia are related to and yet different from Freud's life instinct and death instinct. They are also related to another important concept of Freud's which is part of his earlier libido theory, that of the "anal libido" and the "anal character." Freud published one of his most fundamental discoveries in his paper *Character and Anal Eroticism* (*Charakter und Analerotik*), in 1909.[16] He wrote:

The people I am about to describe are noteworthy for a regular combination of the three following characteristics. They are especially *orderly, parsimonious* and *obstinate.* Each of these words actually covers a small group or series of interrelated character-traits. "Orderly" covers the notion of bodily cleanliness, as well as of conscientiousness in carrying out small duties and trustworthiness. Its opposite would be "untidy" and "neglectful." Parsimony may appear in the exaggerated form of avarice; and obstinacy can go over into defiance, to which rage and revengefulness are easily joined. The two latter qualities—parsimony and obstinacy—are linked with each other more closely than they are with the first—with orderliness. They are, also, the more constant element of the whole complex. Yet it seems to me incontestable that all three in some way belong together.[17]

Freud then proceeded to suggest "that these character traits or orderliness, parsimony and obstinacy, which are often prominent in people who were formerly anal erotics, are to be re-

16 Sigmund Freud (Standard Edition; London: Hogarth Press, 1959), Vol. IX.
17 *Ibid.,* p. 169.

garded as the first and most constant results of the sublimation of anal eroticism."[18] Freud, and later other psychoanalysts, showed that other forms of parsimony do not refer to feces but to money, dirt, property, and to the possession of unusable material. It was also pointed out that the anal character often showed traits of sadism and destructiveness. Psychoanalytic research has demonstrated the validity of Freud's discovery with ample clinical evidence. There is, however, a difference of opinion about the theoretical explanation for the phenomenon of the "anal character," or the "hoarding character" as I have called it.[19] Freud, in line with his libido theory, assumed that the energy supplying the anal libido and its sublimation, was related to an erogenous zone (in this case the anus), and that because of constitutional factors together with individual experiences in the process of toilet training, this anal libido remains stronger than is the case in the average person. I differ from Freud's view inasmuch as I do not see sufficient evidence to assume that the anal libido, as one partial drive of the sexual libido, is the dynamic basis for the development of the anal character.

My own experience in the study of the anal character has led me to believe that we deal here with persons who have a deep interest in and affinity to feces as part of their general affinity to all that is not alive. The feces are the product which is finally eliminated by the body, being of no further use to it. The anal character is attracted by feces as he is attracted by everything which is useless for life, such as dirt, useless things, property merely as possession and not as the means for production and consumption. As to causes for the development of this attraction to what is not alive, there is still much to be studied. We have reason to assume that aside from constitutional factors, the character of the parents, and especially that of the mother, is an important factor. The mother who insists on strict toilet training and who shows an undue interest in the child's processes of evacuation, etc., is a woman with a strong anal character, that is, a strong interest in that which is unalive and

[18] *Ibid.*, p. 171.
[19] Cf. Fromm, *Man For Himself*, pp. 65 ff.

dead, and she will affect the child in the same direction. At the same time she will also lack joy in life; she will not be stimulating, but deadening. Often her anxiety will contribute toward making the child afraid of life and attracted to that which is unalive. In other words, it is not the toilet training as such, with its effects on the anal libido, which leads to the formation of an anal character, but the character of the mother who, by her fear or hate of life, directs interest to the process of evacuation and in many other ways molds the child's energies in the direction of a passion for possessing and hoarding.

It can be easily seen from this description that the anal character in Freud's sense and the necrophilous character as it was described in the foregoing pages, show great similarities. In fact, they are qualitatively alike in their interest in and affinity with the unalive and the dead. They are different only with regard to the intensity of this affinity. I consider the *necrophilous character as being the malignant form of the character structure of which Freud's "anal character" is the benign form*. This implies that there is no sharply defined borderline between the anal and the necrophilous characters, and that many times it will be difficult to determine whether one is dealing with the one or the other.

In the concept of the necrophilous character, a connection is made between Freud's "anal character," which was based on the libido theory, and his purely biological speculation from which the concept of the death instinct resulted. The same link exists between Freud's concept of the "genital character" and his concept of the life instinct, on the one hand, and the biophilic character on the other. This is a first step toward bridging the gap between the earlier and the later theories of Freud, and it is to be hoped that further investigations will help to enlarge this bridge.

Returning now to the *social* conditions for necrophilia, the question arises: What is the relation between necrophilia and the spirit of contemporary industrial society? Furthermore, what is the significance of necrophilia and indifference to life with regard to the motivation for nuclear war?

I shall not concern myself here with *all* the aspects motivating modern war, many of which have existed for previous wars as they do for nuclear war, but only with *one* very crucial psychological problem pertaining to nuclear war. Whatever the rationale of previous wars may have been—defense against attack, economic gain, liberation, glory, the preservation of a way of life—such rationale does not hold true for nuclear war. There is no defense, no gain, no liberation, no glory, when at the very "best" half the population of one's country has been incinerated within hours, all cultural centers have been destroyed, and a barbaric, brutalized life remains in which those still alive will envy the dead.[20]

Why is it that in spite of all this, preparations continue to be made for nuclear war without any more widespread protest than that which exists? How are we to understand why not more people with children and grandchildren do not stand up and protest? Why is it that people who have much to live for, or so it would seem, are soberly considering the destruction of all? There are many answers;[21] yet none of them gives a satisfactory explanation unless we include the following: that *people are not afraid of total destruction because they do not love life;* or because *they are indifferent to life,* or even because *many are attracted to death.*

This hypothesis seems to contradict all our assumptions that people life and are afraid of death; furthermore, that our culture, more than any culture before, provides people with plenty of excitement and fun. But, so we must ask, maybe all

---

[20] I cannot accept those theories which try to persuade us that *(a)* the sudden destruction of sixty million Americans will not have a profound and devastating influence on our civilization or *(b)* that even after nuclear war has started, such rationality will continue to exist among the enemies that they will conduct the war according to a set of rules which will prevent total destruction.

[21] One important answer seems to lie in the fact that most people are deeply—although mostly unconsciously—anxious in their personal lives. The constant battle to rise on the social ladder and the constant fear of failure create a permanent state of anxiety and stress which make the average person forget the threat to his own and the world's existence.

our fun and excitement are quite different from joy and love of life?

In order to answer these questions I must refer to the previous analysis of the life-loving and death-loving orientations. Life is structured growth, and by its very nature is not subject to strict control or prediction. In the realm of life others can be influenced only by the forces of life, such as love, stimulation, example. Life can be experienced only in its individual manifestations, in the individual person as well as in a bird or a flower. There is no life of "the masses," there is no life in abstraction. Our approach to life today becomes increasingly mechanical. Our main aim is to produce things, and in the process of this idolatry of things we transform ourselves into commodities. People are treated as numbers. The question here is not whether they are treated nicely and are well fed (things, too, can be treated nicely); the question is whether people are things or living beings. People love mechanical gadgets more than living beings. The approach to men is intellectual-abstract. One is interested in people as objects, in their common properties, in the statistical rules of mass behavior, not in living individuals. All this goes together with the increasing role of bureaucratic methods. In giant centers of production, giant cities, giant countries, men are administered as if they were things; men and their administrators are transformed into things, and they obey the laws of things. But man is not meant to be a thing; he is destroyed if he becomes a thing; and before this is accomplished he becomes desperate and wants to kill all life.

In a bureaucratically organized and centralized industrialism, tastes are manipulated so that people consume maximally and in predictable and profitable directions. Their intelligence and character become standardized by the ever increasing role of tests which select the mediocre and unadventurous in preference to the original and daring. Indeed, the bureaucratic-industrial civilization which has been victorious in Europe and North America has created a new type of man; he can be described as the *organization man,* as the *automaton man,* and as *homo consumens.* He is, in addition, *homo mechanicus;* by this I mean a gadget man, deeply attracted by all that is mechanical, and inclined against that which is alive. It is true that man's biological and physiological equipment provides him with such strong sexual impulses that even *homo mechanicus* still has sexual desires and looks for women. But there is no doubt that the gadget man's interest in women is diminishing. A New Yorker cartoon pointed to this very amusingly; a salesgirl trying to sell a certain brand of perfume to a young female customer recommends it by remarking: "It smells like a new sports-car." Indeed, any observer of male behavior today will confirm that this cartoon is more than a clever joke. There are apparently a great number of men who are more interested in sports cars, television and radio sets, space travel, and any number of gadgets than they are in women, love, nature, food; who are more stimulated by the manipulation of nonorganic, mechanical things than by life. It is not even too far-fetched to assume that *homo mechanicus* is more proud of and fascinated by devices which can kill millions of people across a distance of several thousand miles within minutes, than he is frightened of and depressed by the possibility of such mass destruction. *Homo mechanicus* still enjoys sex and drink. But all these pleasures are sought within the frame of reference of the mechanical and unalive. He expects that there must be a button which, if pushed, will bring happiness, love, pleasure. (Many go to a psychoanalyst under the illusion that he can teach them where to find the button.) He looks at women as one would at a car: he knows the right buttons to push, he enjoys his power to make her "race" and he remains the cold, watching observer. *Homo mechanicus* becomes more and more interested in the manipulation of machines rather than in participation in and response to life. Hence he becomes indifferent to life, fascinated by the mechanical, and eventually attracted by death and total destruction.

Consider the role that killing plays in our amusements. The movies, the comic strips, the newspapers are full of excitement because they are full of reports of destruction, sadism, brutality. Millions of people live humdrum but comfortable existences—and nothing excites them more than to see or read of killings, whether it is murder or a fatal accident in an automobile race. Is this not an indication of how deep this fascination with death has already become? Or think of expressions such as being "thrilled to death" or "dying to" do this or that, or the expression "it kills me". Consider the indifference to life which is manifested in our rate of automobile accidents.

Briefly then, intellectualization, quantification, abstractification, bureaucratization, and reification—the very characteristics of modern industrial society, when applied to people rather than to things, are not the principles of life but those of mechanics. People living in such a system become indifferent to life and even attracted to death. They are not aware of this. They take the thrills of excitement for the joys of life and live under the illusion that they are very much alive when they have many things to own and to use. The lack of protest against nuclear war, the discussions of our "atomologists" of the balance sheet of total or half-total destruction, shows how far we have already gone into the "valley of the shadow of death."

These features of a necrophilous orientation exist in all modern industrial societies, regardless of their respective political structures. What Soviet state-capitalism has in common in this respect with corporate capitalism is more important than the features in which the systems differ. Both systems have in common the bureaucratic-mechanical approach, and both are preparing for total destruction.

The affinity between the necrophilous contempt for life and the admiration for speed and all that is mechanical has become apparent only in the last decades. Yet as early as in 1909 it was seen and succinctly expressed by Marinetti in his *Initial Manifesto of Futurism:*

1. We shall sing the love of danger, the habit of energy and boldness.

2. The essential elements of our poetry shall be courage, daring and rebellion.

3. Literature has hitherto glorified thoughtful immobility, ecstasy and sleep; we shall extol aggressive movement, feverish insomnia, the double quick step, the somersault, the box on the ear, the fisticuff.

4. We declare that the world's splendour has been enriched by a

new beauty; the beauty of speed. A racing motor-car, its frame adorned with great pipes, like snakes with explosive breath . . . a roaring motor-car, which looks as though running on a shrapnel is more beautiful than the *Victory of Samothrace.*

5. We shall sing of the man at the steering wheel, whose ideal stem transfixes the Earth, rushing over the circuit of her orbit.

6. The poet must give himself with frenzy, with splendour and with lavishness, in order to increase the enthusiastic fervour of the primordial elements.

7. There is no more beauty except in strife. No master-piece without aggressiveness. Poetry must be a violent onslaught upon the unknown forces, to command them to bow before man.

8. We stand upon the extreme promontory of the centuries! . . . Why should we look behind us, when we have to break in the mysterious portals of the Impossible? Time and Space died yesterday. Already we live in the absolute, since we have already created speed, eternal and ever-present.

9. We wish to glorify war—the only health giver of the world—militarism, patriotism, the destructive arm of the Anarchist, the beautiful Ideas that kill, the contempt for woman.

10. We wish to destroy the museums, the libraries, to fight against moralism, feminism and all opportunistic and utilitarian meannesses.

11. We shall sing of the great crowds in the excitement of labour, pleasure and rebellion; of the multi-coloured and polyphonic surf of revolutions in modern capital cities; of the nocturnal vibration of arsenals and workshops beneath their violent electric moons; of the greedy stations swallowing smoking snakes; of factories suspended from the clouds by their strings of smoke; of bridges leaping like gymnasts over the diabolical cutlery of sunbathed rivers; of adventurous liners scenting the horizon; of broad-chested locomotives prancing on the rails, like huge steel horses bridled with long tubes; and of the gliding flight of aeroplanes, the sound of whose screw is like the flapping of flags and the applause of an enthusiastic crowd.[22]

It is interesting to compare Marinetti's necrophilous interpretation of technique and industry with the deeply biophilous interpretation to be found in Walt Whitman's poems. At the end of his poem "Crossing Brooklyn Ferry" he says:

Thrive, cities—bring your freight, bring your shows, ample and sufficient rivers,
Expand, being than which none else is perhaps more spiritual,
Keep your places, objects than which none else is more lasting.

[22] Joshua C. Taylor, *Futurism,* Doubleday Co., 1909, p. 124.

You have waited, you always wait, you dumb, beautiful ministers,
We receive you with free sense at last, and are insatiate henceforward,
Not you any more shall be able to foil us, or withhold yourselves
    from us,
We use you, and do not cast you aside—we plant you permanently
    within us,
We fathom you not—we love you—there is perfection in you also,
You furnish your parts toward eternity,
Great or small, you furnish your parts toward the soul.

Or at the end of the "Song of the Open Road":

> Camerado, I give you my hand!
> I give you my love more precious than money,
> I give you myself before preaching or law;
> Will you give me yourself? Will you come travel with me?
> Shall we stick by each other as long as we live?

Whitman could not have expressed his opposition to necrophilia better than in this line: "To pass on (oh living, always
living!) and leave the corpses behind."

If we compare Marinetti's attitude toward industry with that
of Walt Whitman, it becomes clear that industrial production as
such is not necessarily contrary to the principles of life. The
question is whether the principles of life are subordinated to those
of mechanization, or whether the principles of life are the dominant ones. Obviously, so far the industrialized world has not found
an answer to the question which is posed here: How is it possible
to create a humanist industrialism as against the bureaucratic
industrialism which rules our lives today?

IV
Individual and Social Narcissism

One of the most fruitful and far-reaching of Freud's discoveries is his concept of narcissism. Freud himself considered it to be one of his most important findings, and employed it for the understanding of such distinct phenomena as psychosis ("narcissistic neurosis"), love, castration fear, jealousy, sadism, and also for the understanding of mass phenomena, such as the readiness of the suppressed classes to be loyal to their rulers. In this chapter I want to continue along Freud's line of thought and examine the role of narcissism for the understanding of nationalism, national hatred, and the psychological motivations for destructiveness and war.

I want to mention in passing the fact that the concept of narcissism found hardly any attention in the writings of Jung and Adler, and also less than it deserves in those of Horney. Even in orthodox Freudian theory and therapy the use of the concept of narcissism has remained very much restricted to the narcissism of the infant and that of the psychotic patient. It is probably due to the fact that Freud forced his concept into the frame of his libido theory that the fruitfulness of the concept has not been sufficiently appreciated.

Freud started out with his concern to understand schizophrenia in terms of the libido theory. Since the schizophrenic patient does not seem to have any libidinous relationship to objects (either in fact or in fantasy) Freud was led to the question: "What has happened to the libido which has been withdrawn from external objects in schizophrenia?"[1] His answer is: "The libido that has been withdrawn from the external world has been directed to the ego and thus gives rise to an attitude which may be called narcissism."[2] Freud assumed that the libido is originally all stored in the ego, as though in a "great reservoir," then extended to objects, but easily withdrawn from them and returned to the ego. This view was changed in 1922 when Freud wrote that "we must recognize the id as the great reservoir of the libido," although he never seems to have abandoned entirely the earlier view.[3]

However, the theoretical question whether the libido starts originally in the ego or in the id is of no substantial importance for the meaning of the concept itself. Freud never altered the basic idea that the original state of man, in early infancy, is that of narcissism ("primary narcissism") in which there are not yet any relations to the outside world, that then in the course of normal development the child begins to increase in scope and intensity his (libidinal) relationships to the outside world, but that in many instances (the most drastic one being insanity), he withdraws his libidinal attachment from objects and directs it back to his ego ("secondary narcissism"). But even in the case of normal development, man remains to some extent narcissistic throughout his life.[4]

What is the development of narcissism in the "normal" person? Freud sketched the main lines of this development, and the following paragraph is a short summary of his findings.

The fetus in the womb still lives in a state of absolute narcissism. "By being born", says Freud, "we have made the step from an absolutely self-sufficient narcissism to the perception of a changing external world and the beginning of the discovery of objects."[5] It takes months before the infant can even perceive objects outside as such, as being part of the "not me." By many

---

[1] Freud, *On Narcissism* (Standard Edition; London: Hogarth Press, 1959), Vol. XIV, p. 74.

[2] *Ibid.*, p. 75.

[3] See the discussion of this development in Freud, *Appendix B,* Standard Edition, Vol. XIX, pp. 63 ff.

[4] Freud, *Totem and Taboo* (Standard Edition), Vol. XIII, pp. 88-89.

[5] Freud, *Group Psychology* (Standard Edition), Vol. XVIII, p. 130.

blows to the child's narcissism, his ever increasing acquaintance with the outside world and its laws, thus of "necessity," man develops his original narcissism into "object love." But, says Freud, "a human being remains to some extent narcissistic even after he has found external objects for his libido."[6] Indeed, the development of the individual can be defined in Freud's term as the evolution from absolute narcissism to a capacity for objective reasoning and object love, a capacity, however, which does not transcend definite limitations. The "normal," "mature" person is one whose narcissism has been reduced to the socially accepted minimum without ever disappearing completely. Freud's observation is confirmed by everyday experience. It seems that in most people one can find a narcissistic core which is not accessible and which defies any attempt at complete dissolution.

Those not sufficiently acquainted with Freud's technical language will probably not obtain a distinct idea of the reality and power of narcissism, unless some more concrete description of the phenomenon is forthcoming. This I shall try to give in the following pages. Before I do so, however, I wish to clarify something about the terminology. Freud's views on narcissism are based on his concept of sexual libido. As I have already indicated, this mechanistic libido concept proved more to block than to further the development of the concept of narcissism. I believe that the possibilities of bringing it to its full fruition are much greater if one uses a concept of psychic energy which is not identical with the energy of the *sexual* drive. This was done by Jung; it even found some initial recognition in Freud's idea of desexualized libido. But although nonsexual psychic energy differs from Freud's libido it is, like libido an *energy* concept; it deals with psychic forces, visible only through their manifestations, which have a certain intensity and a certain direction. This energy binds, unifies, and holds together the individual within himself as well as the individual in his relationship to the world outside. Even if one does not agree with Freud in his earlier view that aside from the drive for survival, the energy of the sexual instinct (libido)

[6] Freud, *Totem and Taboo* (Standard Edition), Vol. XIII, p. 89.

is the only important motive power for human conduct, and if one uses instead a general concept of psychic energy, the difference is not as great as many who think in dogmatic terms are prone to believe. The essential point on which any theory or therapy which could be called psychoanalysis depends, is the *dynamic concept of human behavior; that is, the assumption that highly charged forces motivate behavior, and that behavior can be understood and predicted only by understanding* these forces. This dynamic concept of human behavior is the center of Freud's system. How these forces are theoretically conceived, whether in terms of a mechanistic-materialistic philosophy or in terms of humanistic realism, is an important question, but one which is secondary to the central issue of the dynamic interpretation of human behavior.

Let us begin our description of narcissism with two extreme examples: the "primary narcissism" of the newborn infant, and the narcissism of the insane person. The infant is not yet related to the outside world (in Freudian terminology his libido has not yet cathexed outside objects). Another way of putting it is to say that the outside world does not exist for the infant, and this to such a degree that it is not able to distinguish between the "I" and the "not I". We might also say that the infant is not "inter-ested" (inter-esse) = "to be in") in the world outside. The only reality that exists for the infant is itself: its body, its physical sensations of cold and warmth, thirst, need for sleep and bodily contact.

The insane person is in a situation not essentially different from that of the infant. But while for the infant the world outside has *not yet emerged* as real, for the insane person it *has ceased* to be real. In the case of hallucinations, for instance, the senses have lost their function of registering outside events—they register subjective experience in categories of sensory response to objects outside. In the paranoid delusion the same mechanism operates. Fear or suspicion, for instance, which are subjective emotions, become objectified in such a way that the paranoid person is convinced that others are conspiring against him; this is precisely the difference to the neurotic person: the latter may be constantly afraid of being hated, persecuted, etc., but he still knows that this is what he *fears*. For the paranoid person the fear has been transformed into a fact.

A particular instance of narcissism which lies on the borderline between sanity and insanity can be found in some men who have reached an extraordinary degree of power. The Egyptian pharaohs, the Roman Caesars, the Borgias, Hitler, Stalin, Trujillo—they all show certain similar features. They have attained absolute power; their word is the ultimate judgment of everything, including life and death; there seems to be no limit to their capacity to do what they want. They are gods, limited only by illness, age and death. They try to find a solution to the problem of human existence by the desperate attempt to transcend the limitation of human existence. They try to pretend that there is no limit to their lust and to their power, so they sleep with countless women, they kill numberless men, they build castles everywhere, they "want the moon," they "want the impossible."[7] This is madness, even though it is an attempt to solve the problem of existence by pretending that one is not human. It is a madness which tends to grow in the lifetime of the afflicted person. The more he tries to be god, the more he isolates himself from the human race; this isolation makes him more frightened, everybody becomes his enemy, and in order to stand the resulting fright he has to increase his power, his ruthlessness, and his narcissism. This Caesarian madness would be nothing but plain insanity were it not for one factor: by his power Caesar has bent reality to his narcissistic fantasies. He has forced everybody to agree that he is god, the most powerful and the wisest of men—hence his own megalomania seems to be a reasonable feeling. On the other hand, many will hate him, try to overthrow and kill him—hence his pathological suspicions are also backed by a nucleus of reality. As a result he does not feel disconnected from reality—hence he can keep a modicum of sanity, even though in a precarious state.

Psychosis is a state of absolute narcissism, one in which the person has broken all connection with reality outside, and has

---

[7] Camus, in his drama *Caligula*, has portrayed this madness of power most accurately.

made his own person the substitute for reality. He is entirely filled with himself, he has become "god and the world" to himself. It is precisely this insight by which Freud for the first time opened the way to the dynamic understanding of the nature of psychosis.

However, for those who are not familiar with psychosis it is necessary to give a picture of narcissism as it is found in neurotic or "normal" persons. One of the most elementary examples of narcissism can be found in the average person's attitude toward his own body. Most people like their own body, their face, their figure, and when asked whether they would want to change with another perhaps more handsome person, very definitely say no. Even more telling is the fact that most people do not mind at all the sight or smell of their own feces (in fact, some like them), while they have a definite aversion for those of other people. Quite obviously there is no aesthetic or other judgment involved here; the same thing which when connected with one's own body is pleasant, is unpleasant when connected with somebody else's.

Let us now take another and less common example of narcissism. A man calls the doctor's office and wants an appointment. The doctor says that he cannot make an appointment for that same week, and suggests a date for the following. The patient insists on his request for an early appointment, and as an explanation does not say, as one might expect, why there is such urgency, but mentions the fact that he lives only five minutes away from the doctor's office. When the doctor answers that his own time problem is not solved by the fact that it takes so little time for the patient to come to his office, the latter shows no understanding; he continues to insist that he has given a good enough reason for the doctor to give him an earlier appointment. If the doctor is a psychiatrist he will already have made a significant diagnostic observation, namely, that he is dealing here with an extremely narcissistic person, that is to say, with a very sick person. The reasons are not difficult to see. The patient is not able to see the doctor's situation as something apart from his own. All that is in his, the patient's, field of vision is his own wish to see the doctor, and the fact that for *him* it takes little time to come. The doctor as a separate person with his own schedule and needs does not exist. The patient's logic is that if it is easy for him to come, then it is easy for the doctor to see him. The diagnostic observation about the patient would be somewhat different if, after the doctor's first explanation, the patient were able to answer, "Oh, doctor, of course, I see; I am sorry, that really was kind of a stupid thing for me to say." In this case we would also be dealing with a narcissistic person who at first does not differentiate between his own and the doctor's situation, but his narcissism is not as intensive and rigid as that of the first patient. He is able to see the reality of the situation when his attention is called to it, and he responds accordingly. This second patient would probably be embarrassed about his blunder once he saw it; the first one would not be embarrassed at all—he would only feel critical of the doctor who was too stupid to see such a simple point.

A similar phenomenon can easily be observed in a narcissistic man who falls in love with a woman who does not respond. The narcissistic person will be prone not to believe that the woman does not love him. He will reason: "It is impossible that she does not love me when I love her so much," or "I could not love her so much if she did not love me too." He then proceeds to rationalize the woman's lack of response by suppositions such as these: "She loves me unconsciously; she is afraid of the intensity of her own love; she wants to test me, to torture me"—and whatnot. The essential point here, as in the previous case, is that the narcissistic person cannot perceive the reality within another person as distinct from his own.

Let us look at two phenomena which are apparently extremely different, and yet both of which are narcissistic. A woman spends many hours every day before the mirror to fix her hair and face. It is not simply that she is vain. She is obsessed with her body and her beauty, and her body is the only important reality she knows. She comes perhaps nearest to the Greek legend which speaks of Narcissus, a beautiful lad who rejected the love of the nymph Echo, who died of a broken heart. Nemesis punished him by making him fall in love with the reflection of his own image in the water of the lake; in self-admiration he fell into the lake and died.

The Greek legend indicates clearly that this kind of "self-love" is a curse, and that in its extreme form it ends in self-destruction.[8] Another woman (and it could well be the same one some years later) suffers from hypochondriasis. She is also constantly preoccupied with her body although not in the sense of making it beautiful, but in fearing illness. Why the positive, or the negative, image is chosen has, of course, its reasons; however, we need not deal with these here. What matters is that behind both phenomena lies the same narcissistic preoccupation with oneself, with little interest left for the outside world.

Moral hypochondriasis is not essentially different. Here the person is not afraid of being sick and of dying, but of being guilty. Such a person is constantly preoccupied with his guilt about things he has done wrong, with sins he has committed, etc. While to the outsider—and to himself—he may appear to be particularly conscientious, moral, and even concerned with others, the fact is that such a person is concerned only with himself, with his conscience, with what others might say about him, etc. The narcissism underlying physical or moral hypochondriasis is the same as the narcissism of the vain person, except that it is less apparent, as such, to the untrained eye. One finds this kind of narcissism, which has been classified by K. Abraham as *negative narcissism,* particularly in states of melancholia, characterized by feelings of inadequacy, unreality, and self-accusation.

In still less drastic forms one can see the narcissistic orientation in daily life. A well-known joke expresses it nicely. A writer meets a friend and talks to him a long time about himself; he then says: "I have talked so long about myself. Let us now talk about *you.* How did you like my latest book?" This man is typical of many who are preoccupied with themselves and who pay little attention to others, except as echoes of themselves. Often even if they act helpfully and kind, they do so because they like to see themselves in this role; their energy is taken up with admiring themselves

[8] Cf. my discussion of self-love in *Man for Himself.* I try to show there that true love for self is not different from love for others; that "self-love" in the sense of egoistic, narcissistic love is to be found in those who can love neither others nor themselves.

rather than with realizing things from the point of view of the person they are helping.

How does one recognize the narcissistic person? There is one type which is easily recognized. That is the kind of person who shows all the signs of self-satisfaction; one can see that when he says some trivial words he feels as if he has said something of great importance. He usually does not listen to what others say, nor is he really interested. (If he is clever, he will try to hide this fact by asking questions and making it a point to seem interested.) One can also recognize the narcissistic person by his sensitivity to any kind of criticism. This sensitivity can be expressed by denying the validity of any criticism, or by reacting with anger or depression. In many instances the narcissistic orientation may be hidden behind an attitude of modesty and humility; in fact, it is not rare for a person's narcissistic orientation to take his humility as the object of his self-admiration. Whatever the different manifestations of narcissism are, a lack of genuine interest in the outside world is common to all forms of narcissism.[9]

Sometimes the narcissistic person can also be recognized by his facial expression. Often we find a kind of glow or smile, which gives the impression of smugness to some, of beatific, trusting, childlikeness to others. Often the narcissism, especially in its most extreme forms, manifests itself in a peculiar glitter in the eyes, taken by some as a symptom of half-saintliness, by others of half-craziness. Many very narcissistic persons talk incessantly—often at a meal, where they forget to eat and thus make everyone else wait. Company or food are less important than their "ego."

The narcissistic person has not even necessarily taken his whole

---

[9] Sometimes it is not easy to distinguish between the vain, narcissistic person and one with a low self-evaluation; the latter often is in need of praise and admiration, not because he is not interested in anyone else, but because of his self-doubts and low self-evaluation. There is another important distinction which is also not always easy to make: that between narcissism and egotism. Intense narcissism implies an inability to experience reality in its fullness; intense egotism implies to have little concern, love or sympathy for others but it does not necessarily imply the overevaluation of one's subjective processes. In other words the extreme egotist is not necessarily extremely narcissistic; selfishness is not necessarily blindness to objective reality.

person as the object of his narcissism. Often he has cathexed a partial aspect of his personality with his narcissism; for instance, his honor, his intelligence, his physical prowess, his wit, his good looks (sometimes even narrowed down to such details as his hair or his nose). Sometimes his narcissism refers to qualities about which normally a person would not be proud, such as his capacity to be afraid and thus to foretell danger. "He" becomes identified with a partial aspect of himself. If we ask who "he" is, the proper answer would be that "he" is his brain, his fame, his wealth, his penis, his conscience, and so on. All the idols of the various religions represent so many partial aspects of man. In the narcissistic person the object of his narcissism is any one of these partial qualities which constitute for him his self. The one whose self is represented by his property can take very well a threat to his dignity, but a threat to his property is like a threat to his life. On the other hand, for the one whose self is represented by his intelligence, the fact of having said something stupid is so painful that it may result in a mood of serious depression. However, the more intense the narcissism is, the less will the narcissistic person accept the fact of failure on his side, or any legitimate criticism from others. He will just feel outraged by the insulting behavior of the other person, or believe that the other person is too insensitive, uneducated, etc., to have proper judgment. (I think, in this connection, of a brilliant, yet highly narcissistic man who, when confronted with the results of a Rorschach test he had taken and which fell short of the ideal picture he had of himself, said, "I am sorry for the psychologist who did this test; he must be very paranoid.")

We must now mention one other factor which complicates the phenomenon of narcissism. Just as the narcissistic person has made his "self-image" the object of his narcissistic attachment, he does the same with everything connected with him. *His* ideas, *his* knowledge, *his* house, but also people in *his* "sphere of interest" become objects of his narcissistic attachment. As Freud pointed out, the most frequent example is probably the narcissistic attachment to one's children. Many parents believe that their own children are the most beautiful, intelligent, etc., in comparison with other children. It seems that the younger the children are, the more intense is this narcissistic bias. The parents' love, and especially the mother's love for the infant, is to a considerable extent love for the infant as an extension of oneself. Adult love between man and woman also has often a narcissistic quality. The man who is in love with a woman may transfer his narcissism to her once she has become "his." He admires and worships her for qualities which he has conferred upon her; precisely because of her being part of him, she becomes the bearer of extraordinary qualities. Such a man will often also think that all things he possesses are extraordinarily wonderful, and he will be "in love" with them.

Narcissism is a passion the intensity of which in many individuals can only be compared with sexual desire and the desire to stay alive. In fact, many times it proves to be stronger than either. Even in the average individual in whom it does not reach such intensity, there remains a narcissistic core which appears to be almost indestructible. This being so we might suspect that like sex and survival, the narcissistic passion also has an important *biological function*. Once we raise this question the answer comes readily. How could the individual survive unless his bodily needs, his interests, his desires, were charged with much energy? Biologically, from the standpoint of survival, man must attribute to himself an importance far above what he gives to anybody else. If he did not do so, from where would he take the energy and interest to defend himself against others, to work for his subsistence, to fight for his survival, to press his claims against those of others? Without narcissism he might be a saint—but do saints have a high survival rate? What from a spiritual standpoint would be most desirable—absence of narcissism—would be most dangerous from the mundane standpoint of survival. Speaking teleologically, we can say that nature had to endow man with a great amount of narcissism to enable him to do what is necessary for survival. This is true especially because nature has not endowed man with well-developed instincts such as the animal has. The animal has no "problems" of survival in the sense that its built-in instinctive nature takes care of survival in such a way that the animal does not have to consider or decide whether or not it wants to make an effort. In man the instinctive apparatus has lost most of its efficacy—hence narcissism assumes a very necessary biological function.

However, once we recognize that narcissism fulfills an important biological function, we are confronted with another question. Does not extreme narcissism have the function of making man indifferent to others, incapable of giving second place to his own needs when this is necessary for co-operation with others? Does not narcissism make man asocial and, in fact, when it reaches an extreme degree, insane? There can be no doubt that extreme individual narcissism would be a severe obstacle to all social life. But if this is so, narcissism must be said to be in *conflict* with the principle of survival, for the individual can survive only if he organizes himself in groups; hardly anyone would be able to protect himself all alone against the dangers of nature, nor would he be able to do many kinds of work which can only be done in groups.

We arrive then at the paradoxical result that narcissism is necessary for survival, and at the same time that it is a threat to survival. The solution of this paradox lies in two directions. One is that *optimal* rather than *maximal* narcissism serves survival; that is to say, the biologically necessary degree of narcissism is reduced to the degree of narcissism that is compatible with social co-operation. The other lies in the fact that individual narcissism is transformed into group narcissism, that the clan, nation, religion, race, etc., become the objects of narcissistic passion instead of the individual. Thus, narcissistic energy is maintained but used in the interests of the survival of the group rather than for the survival of the individual. Before I deal with this problem of group narcissism and its sociological function, I want to discuss the *pathology of narcissism*.

The most dangerous result of narcissistic attachment is the distortion of rational judgment. The object of narcissistic attachment is thought to be valuable (good, beautiful, wise, etc.) not on the basis of an objective value-judgment, but because it is me or mine. Narcissistic value-judgment is prejudiced and biased. Usually this prejudice is rationalized in one form or another, and this rationalization may be more or less deceptive according to the intelligence and sophistication of the person involved. In the drunkard's narcissism the distortion is usually obvious. What we see is a man who talks in a superficial and banal way, yet with the air and intonation of one voicing the most wonderful and interesting words. Subjectively he has a euphoric "on-top-of-the-world" feeling, while in reality he is in a state of self-inflation. All this does not mean to say that the highly narcissistic person's utterances are necessarily boring. If he is gifted or intelligent he will produce interesting ideas, and if he evaluates them highly, his judgment will not be entirely wrong. But the narcissistic person tends to evaluate his own productions highly anyway, and their real quality is not decisive in reaching this evaluation. (In the case of "negative narcissism" the opposite is true. Such a person tends to underevaluate everything that is his own, and his judgment is equally biased.) If he were aware of the distorted nature of his narcissistic judgments, the results would not be so bad. He would—and could—take a humorous attitude toward his narcissistic bias. But this is rare. Usually the person is convinced that there is no bias, and that his judgment is objective and realistic. This leads to a severe distortion of his capacity to think and to judge, since this capacity is blunted again and again when he deals with himself and what is his. Correspondingly, the narcissistic person's judgment is also biased against that which is not "he" or not his. The extraneous ("not me") world is inferior, dangerous, immoral. The narcissistic person then, ends up with an enormous distortion. He and his are overevaluated. Everything outside is underevaluated. The damage to reason and objectivity is obvious.

An ever more dangerous pathological element in narcissism is the emotional reaction to criticism of any narcissistically cathexed position. Normally a person does not become angry when something he has done or said is criticized, provided the criticism is fair and not made with hostile intent. The narcissistic person, on the other hand, reacts with intense anger when he is criticized. He tends to feel that the criticism is a hostile attack, since by the very nature of his narcissism he can not imagine that it is justified.

The intensity of his anger can be fully understood only if one considers that the narcissistic person is unrelated to the world, and as a consequence is alone, and hence frightened. It is this sense of aloneness and fright which is compensated for by his narcissistic self-inflation. If he *is* the world, there is no world outside which can frighten him; if he is everything, he is not alone; consequently, when his narcissism is wounded he feels threatened in his whole existence. When the one protection against his fright, his self-inflation, is threatened, the fright emerges and results in intense fury. This fury is all the more intense because nothing can be done to diminish the threat by appropriate action; only the destruction of the critic—or oneself—can save one from the threat to one's narcissistic security.

There is an alternative to explosive rage as a result of wounded narcissism, and that is *depression*. The narcissistic person gains his sense of identity by inflation. The world outside is not a problem for him, it does not overwhelm him with its power, because he has succeeded in being the world, in feeling omniscient and omnipotent. If his narcissism is wounded, and if for a number of reasons, such as for instance the subjective or objective weakness of his position *vis-à-vis* his critic, he cannot afford to become furious, he becomes depressed. He is unrelated to and uninterested in the world; he is nothing and nobody, since he has not developed his self as the center of his relatedness to the world. If his narcissism is so severely wounded that he can no longer maintain it, his ego collapses and the subjective reflex of this collapse is the feeling of depression. The element of mourning in melancholia refers, in my opinion to the narcissistic image of the wonderful "I" which has died, and for which the depressed person is mourning.

It is precisely because this narcissistic person dreads the depression which results from a wounding of his narcissism that he desperately tries to avoid such wounds. There are several ways of accomplishing this. One is to increase the narcissism in order that no outside criticism or failure can really touch the narcissistic position. In other words, the intensity of narcissism increases in order to ward off the threat. This means, of course, that the person tries to cure himself of the threatening depression by becoming more severely sick mentally, up to the point of psychosis.

There is, however, still another solution to the threat to narcissism which is more satisfactory to the individual, although more dangerous to others. This solution consists in the attempt to transform reality in such a way as to make it conform, to some extent, with his narcissistic self-image. An example of this is the narcissistic inventor who believes he has invented a *perpetuum mobile,* and who in the process has made a minor discovery of some significance. A more important solution consists in getting the consensus of one other person, and, if possible, in obtaining the consensus of millions. The former case is that of a *folie à deux* (some marriages and friendships rest on this basis), while the latter is that of public figures who prevent the open outbreak of their potential psychosis by gaining the acclaim and consensus of millions of people. The best-known example for this latter case is Hitler. Here was an extremely narcissistic person who probably could have suffered a manifest psychosis had he not succeeded in making millions believe in his won self-image, take his grandiose fantasies regarding the millennium of the "Third Reich" seriously, and even transforming reality in such a way that it seemed proved to his followers that he was right. (After he had failed he had to kill himself, since otherwise the collapse of his narcissistic image would have been truly unbearable.)

There are other examples in history of megalomaniac leaders who "cured" their narcissism by transforming the world to fit it; such people must also try to destroy all critics, since they cannot tolerate the threat which the voice of sanity constitutes for them. From Caligula and Nero to Stalin and Hitler we see that their need to find believers, to transform reality so that it fits their narcissism, and to destroy all critics, is so intense and so desperate precisely because it is an attempt to prevent the outbreak of insanity. Paradoxically, the element of insanity in such leaders makes them also successful. It gives them that certainty and freedom from doubt which is so impressive to the average person. Needless to say, this need to change the world and to win others to share in one's ideas and delusions requires also talents and gifts which the average person, psychotic or nonpsychotic, lacks.

In discussing the pathology of narcissism it is important to distinguish between two forms of narcissism—one *benign*, the other *malignant.* In the benign form, the object of narcissism is the result of a person's effort. Thus, for instance, a person may have a narcissistic pride in his work as a carpenter, as a scientist, or as a farmer. Inasmuch as the object of his narcissism is something he has to work for, his exclusive interest in what is *his* work and *his* achievement is constantly balanced by his interest in the process of work itself, and the material he is working with. The dynamics of this benign narcissism thus are self-checking. The energy which propells the work is, to a large extent, of a narcissistic nature, but the very fact that the work itself makes it necessary to be related to reality, constantly curbs the narcissism and keeps it within bounds. This mechanism may explain why we find so many narcissistic people who are at the same time highly creative.

In the case of malignant narcissism, the object of narcissism is not anything the person does or produces, but something he *has;* for instance, his body, his looks, his health, his wealth, etc. The malignant nature of this type of narcissism lies in the fact that it lacks the corrective element which we find in the benign form. If I am "great" because of some quality I *have,* and not because of something I *achieve,* I do not need to be related to anybody or anything; I need not make any effort. In maintaining the picture of my greatness I remove myself more and more from reality and I have to increase the narcissistic charge in order to be better protected from the danger that my narcissistically inflated ego might be revealed as the product of my empty imagination. Malignant narcissism, thus, is not self-limiting, and in consequence it is crudely solipsistic as well as xenophobic. One who has learned to achieve cannot help acknowledging that others have achieved similar things in similar ways—even if his narcissism may persuade him that his own achievement is greater than that of others. One who has achieved nothing will find it difficult to appreciate the achievements of others, and thus he will be forced to isolate himself increasingly in narcissistic splendor.

We have so far described the dynamics of individual narcissism: the phenomenon, its biological function, and its pathology. This description ought to enable us now to understand the phenomenon of _social narcissism_ and the role it plays as a source of violence and war.

The central point of the following discussion is the phenomenon of the transformation of personal into group narcissism. We can start with an observation about the sociological function of group narcissism which parallels the biological function of individual narcissism. From the standpoint of any organized group which wants to survive, it is important that the group be invested by its members with narcissistic energy. The survival of a group depends to some extent on the fact that its members consider its importance as great as or greater than that of their own lives, and furthermore that they believe in the righteousness, or even superiority, of their group as compared with others. Without such narcissistic cathexis of the group, the energy necessary for serving the group, or even making severe sacrifices for it, would be greatly diminished.

In the dynamics of group narcissism we find phenomena similar to those we discussed already in connection with individual narcissism. Here too we can distinguish between benign and malignant forms of narcissism. If the object of group narcissism is an achievement, the same dialectical process takes place which we discussed above. The very need to achieve something creative makes it necessary to leave the closed circle of group solipsism and to be interested in the object it wants to achieve. (If the achievement which a group seeks is conquest, the beneficial effect of truly productive effort will of course be largely absent.) If, on the other hand, group narcissism has as its object the group as it is, its splendor, its past achievements, the physique of its members, then the countertendencies mentioned above will not develop, and the narcissistic orientation and subsequent dangers will steadily increase. In reality, of course, both elements are often blended.

There is another sociological function of group narcissism which has not been discussed so far. A society which lacks the means to provide adequately for the majority of its members, or a large proportion of them, must provide these members with a narcissistic satisfaction of the malignant type if it wants to prevent dissatisfaction among them. For those who are economically and culturally poor, narcissistic pride in belonging to the group is the only—and often a very effective—source of satisfaction. Precisely because life is not "interesting" to them, and does not offer them possibilities for developing interests, they may develop an extreme form of narcissism. Good examples of this phenomenon in recent years are the racial narcissism which existed in Hitler's Germany, and which is found in the American South today. In both instances the core of the racial superiority feeling was, and still is, the lower middle class; this backward class, which in Germany as well as in the American South has been economically and culturally deprived, without any realistic hope of changing its situation (because they are the remnants of an older and dying form of society) has only one satisfaction: the inflated image of itself as the most admirable group in the world, and of being superior to another racial group that is singled out as inferior. The member of such a backward group feels: "Even though I am poor and uncultured I am somebody important because I belong to the most admirable group in the world—I am white"; or, "I am an Aryan."

Group narcissism is less easy to recognize than individual narcissism. Assuming a person tells others, "I (and my family) are the most admirable people in the world; we alone are clean, intelligent, good, decent; all others are dirty, stupid, dishonest and irresponsible," most people would think him crude, unbalanced, or even insane. If, however, a fanatical speaker addresses a mass audience, substituting the nation (or race, religion, political party, etc.) for the "I" and "my family," he will be praised and admired by many for his love of country, love of God, etc. Other nations and religions, however, will resent such a speech for the obvious reason that they are held in contempt. *Within* the favored group, however, everybody's personal narcissism is flattered and the fact that millions of people agree with the statements makes them appear as reasonable. (What the majority of people consider to be "reasonable" is that about which there is agreement, if not among all, at least among a substantial number of people; "reasonable," for most people, has nothing to do with reason, but with consensus.) Inasmuch as the group as a whole requires group narcissism for its survival, it will further narcissistic attitudes and confer upon them the qualification of being particularly virtuous.

The group to which the narcissistic attitude is extended has varied in structure and size throughout history. In the primitive tribe or clan it may comprise only a few hundred members; here the individual is not yet an "individual" but is still united to the blood group by "primary bonds"[10] which have not yet been broken. The narcissistic involvement with the clan is thus strengthened by the fact that its members emotionally have still no existence of their own outside of the clan.

In the development of the human race we find an ever increasing range of socialization; the original small group based on blood affinity gives way to ever larger groups based on a common language, a common social order, a common faith. The larger size of the group does not necessarily mean that the pathological qualities of narcissism are reduced. As was remarked earlier, the group narcissism of the "whites" or the "Aryans" is as malignant as the extreme narcissism of a single person can be. Yet in general we find that in the process of socialization which leads to the formation of larger groups, the need for co-operation with many other and different people not connected among themselves by ties of blood, tends to counteract the narcissistic charge within the group. The same holds true in another respect, which we have discussed in connection with benign individual narcissism: inasmuch as the large group (nation, state, or religion) makes it an object of its narcissistic pride to achieve something valuable in the fields of material, intellectual, or artistic production, the very process of work in such fields tends to lessen the narcissistic charge. The history of the Roman Catholic Church is one of many examples of the peculiar mixture of narcissism and the counteracting forces within a large group. The elements counteracting

[10] Cf. the discussion of primary bonds in E. Fromm, *Escape From Freedom* (New York: Holt, Rinehart & Winston, 1941).

narcissism within the Catholic Church are, first of all, the concept of the universality of man and of a "catholic" religion which is no longer the religion of one particular tribe or nation. Second, the idea of personal humility which follows from the idea of God and the denial of idols. The existence of God implies that no man can be God, that no individual can be omniscient or omnipotent. It thus sets a definite limit to man's narcissistic self-idolatry. But at the same time the Church has nourished an intense narcissism; believing that the Church is the only chance of salvation and that the Pope is the Vicar of Christ, its members were able to develop an intense narcissism inasmuch as they were members of such an extraordinary institution. The same occurred in relation to God; while the omniscience and omnipotence of God should have led to man's humility, often the individual identified himself with God and thus developed an extraordinary degree of narcissism in this process of identification.

This same ambiguity between a narcisistic or an antinarcissistic function has occurred in all the other great religions, for example, in Buddhism, Judaism, Islam, and Protestantism. I have mentioned the Catholic religion not only because it is a well-known example, but mainly because the Roman Catholic religion was the basis both for humanism and for violent and fanatical religious narcissism at one and the same historical period: the fifteenth and sixteenth centuries. The humanists within the Church and those outside spoke in the name of a humanism which was the fountainhead of Christianity. Nicholas of Cusa preached religious tolerance for all men (*De pace fidei*); Ficino taught that love is the fundamental force of all creation (*De amore*); Erasmus demanded mutual tolerance and a democratization of the Church; Thomas More, the nonconformist, spoke and died for the principles of universalism and human solidarity; Postel, building on the foundations laid by Nicholas and Erasmus, spoke of global peace and world unity (*De orbis terrae concordia*); Siculo, following Pico della Mirandola, spoke enthusiastically of man's dignity, of his reason and virtue, and of his capacity for self-perfection. These men, with many others growing from the soil of Christian humanism, spoke in the name of universality, brotherliness, dignity, and reason. They fought for tolerance and peace.[11]

Against them stood the forces of fanaticism on both sides; that of Luther and that of the Church. The humanists tried to avoid the catastrophe; eventually the fanatics on both sides won. Religious persecution and war, culminating in the disastrous Thirty Years' War, were a blow to humanist development from which Europe has still not recovered (one cannot help thinking of the analogy of Stalinism, destroying socialist humanism three hundred years later). Looking back to the religious hatred of the sixteenth and seventeenth centuries, its irrationalities are clear. Both sides spoke in the name of God, of Christ, of love, and they differed only in points which, if compared with the general principles, were of secondary importance. Yet they hated each other, and each was passionately convinced that humanity ended at the frontiers of his own religious faith. The essence of this over-estimation of ones' own position and the hate for all who differ from it is narcissism. "We" are admirable; "they" are despicable. "We" are good; "they" are evil. Any criticism of one's own doctrine is a vicious and unbearable attack; criticism of the others' position is a well-meant attempt to help them to return to the truth.

From the Renaissance onward, the two great contradictory forces, group narcissism and humanism, have each developed in its own way. Unfortunately the development of group narcissism has vastly outstripped that of humanism. While it seemed possible in the late Middle Ages and at the time of the Renaissance that Europe was prepared for the emergence of a political and religious humanism, this promise failed to materialize. New forms of group narcissism emerged, and dominated the following centuries. This group narcissism assumed manifold forms: religious, national, racial, political. Protestants against Catholics, French against Germans, whites against blacks, Aryans against non-Aryans, Communists against capitalists; different as the con-

[11] Cf. the excellent work by Friedrich Heer, *Die dritte Kraft* (S. Fischer Verlag, 1960).

tents are, psychologically we deal with the same narcissistic phenomenon and its resulting fanaticism and destructiveness.[12]

While group narcissism grew, its counterpart—humanism— also developed. In the eighteenth and nineteenth centuries— from Spinoza, Leibniz, Rousseau, Herder, Kant, to Goethe and Marx—the thought developed that mankind is one, that each individual carries within himself all of humanity, that there must be no privileged groups claiming that their privileges are based on their intrinsic superiority. The First World War was a severe blow to humanism, and gave rise to an increasing orgy of group narcissism: national hysteria in all the belligerent countries of the First World War, Hitler's racialism, Stalin's party idoliza- tion, Muslim and Hindu religious fanaticism, Western anti- Communist fanaticism. These various manifestations of group narcissism have brought the world to the abyss of total de- struction.

As a reaction to this threat to humanity, a renaissance of humanism can be observed today in all countries and among the representatives of diverse ideologies; there are radical hu- manists among Catholic and Protestant theologians, among social- ist and nonsocialist philosophers. Whether the danger of total destruction, the ideas of the neohumanists and the bonds created between all men by the new means of communication will be sufficient to stop the effects of group narcissism is a question which may determine the fate of mankind.

The growing intensity of group narcissism—only shifting from religious to national, racial, and party narcissism—is, indeed, a surprising phenomenon. First of all because of the devel- opment of the humanist forces since the Renaissance, which we discussed earlier. Furthermore, because of the evolution of scientific thought which undermines narcissism. The scientific

---

[12] There are other more harmless forms of group narcissism directed toward small groups like lodges, small religious sects, "the old school tie," etc. While the degree of narcissism in these cases may not be less than in those of the larger groups, the narcissism is less dangerous simply because the groups involved have little power, and hence little capacity to cause harm.

method requires objectivity and realism, it requires seeing the world as it is, and not distorted by one's own desires and fears. It requires being humble towards the facts of reality, and renouncing all hopes of omnipotence and omniscience. The need for critical thought, experimentation, proof; the attitude of doubting—these are characteristic of scientific endeavor, and they are precisely the methods of thought which tend to counter-act the narcissistic orientation. Undoubtedly the method of scientific thinking has had its effect on the development of contemporary neohumanism, and it is not accidental that most of the outstanding natural scientists of our day are humanists. But the vast majority of men in the West, although they have "learned" the scientific method in school or at the university, never really have been touched by the method of scientific, critical thinking. Even most of the professionals in the field of the natural sciences have remained *technicians,* and have not acquired a *scientific attitude.* For the majority of the population, the scientific method they were taught has had even less sig-nificance. Although it may be said that higher education has tended to soften and to modify personal and group narcissism to some extent, it has not prevented most of the "educated" people from joining enthusiastically the national, racial, and political movements which are the expression of contemporary group narcissism.

It seems that, on the contrary, science has created a new object for narcissism—*technique.* Man's narcissistic pride in being the creator of a formerly undreamed-of world of things, the dis-coverer of radio, television, atomic power, space travel, and even in being the potential destroyer of the entire globe, has given him a new object for narcissistic self-inflation. In studying this whole problem of the development of narcissism in modern his-tory, one is reminded of Freud's statement that Copernicus, Darwin, and he himself deeply wounded man's narcissism by undermining his belief in his unique role in the universe and in his consciousness as being an elementary and irreducible real-ity. But while man's narcissism has been wounded in this man-ner, it has not been as greatly reduced as would appear. He has reacted by transferring his narcissism to other objects: nation, race, political creed, technique.

Concerning the *pathology of group narcissism,* the most obvious and frequent symptom, as in the case of individual narcissism, is a lack of objectivity and rational judgment. If one examines the judgment of the poor whites regarding Negroes, or of the Nazis in regard to Jews, one can easily recognize the distorted character of their respective judgments. Little straws of truth are put together, but the whole which is thus formed consists of falsehoods and fabrications. If political actions are based on narcissistic self-glorifications, the lack of objectivity often leads to disastrous consequences. We have witnessed during the first half of this century two outstanding examples of the consequences of national narcissism. Many years before the First World War it was the official French strategic doctrine to claim that the French army did not need much heavy artillery or a large number of machine guns; the French soldier was supposed to be so endowed with the French virtues of courage and offensive spirit that he needed only his bayonet to defeat the enemy. The fact is that hundreds of thousands of French soldiers were mowed down by German machine guns, and that only German strategic mistakes and later American help saved France from defeat. In the Second World War, Germany made a similar mistake. Hitler, a man of extreme personal narcissism, who stimulated the group narcissism of millions of Germans, overestimated the strength of Germany and underestimated not only the strength of the United States, but also the Russian winter—as had another narcissistic general, Napoleon. In spite of his cleverness, Hitler was not capable of seeing *reality objectively,* because his wish to win and to rule weighed more heavily for him than the realities of armaments and climate.

Group narcissism needs satisfaction just as individual narcissism does. On one level this satisfaction is provided by the common ideology of the superiority of one's group, and the inferiority of all others. In religious groups this satisfaction is easily provided by the assumption that *my* group is the only one which believes in the true God, and hence since *my* God is the only true one, all other groups are made up of misguided unbelievers. But even without reference to God as a witness for one's superiority, group narcissism can arrive at similar conclusions on a secular level. The narcissistic conviction of the superiority of whites over Negroes in parts of the United States and in South Africa demonstrates that there is no restraint to the sense of self-superiority or of the inferiority of another group. However, the satisfaction of these narcissistic self-images of a group requires also a certain degree of confirmation in reality. As long as the whites in Alabama or in South Africa have the power to demonstrate their superiority over the Negroes through social, economic, and political acts of discrimination, their narcissistic beliefs have some element of reality, and thus bolster up the entire narcissistic thought-system. The same held true for the Nazis; there the physical destruction of all Jews had to serve as proof of the superiority of the Aryans (for a sadist the fact that he can kill a man proves that the killer is superior). If, however, the narcissistically inflated group does not have available a minority which is sufficiently helpless to lend itself as an object for narcissistic satisfaction, the group's narcissism will easily lead to the wish for military conquests; this was the path of pan-Germanism and pan-Slavism before 1914. In both cases the respective nations were endowed with the role of being the "chosen nation," superior to all others, and hence justified in attacking those who did not accept their superiority. I do not mean to imply that "the" cause of the First World War was the narcissism of the pan-German and pan-Slavic movements, but their fanaticism was certainly one factor which contributed to the outbreak of the war. Beyond this, however, one must not forget that once a war has started, the various governments try to arouse national narcissism as a necessary psychological condition for the successful waging of the war.

If the narcissism of a group is wounded, then we find the same reaction of rage which we have discussed in connection with individcal narcissism. There are many historical examples for the fact that disparagement of the symbols of group narcissism has often produced rage verging on insanity. Violation of the flag; insults against one's own God, emperor, leader; the loss of a war and of territory—these have often led to violent mass feelings of vengeance which in turn led to new wars. The wounded narcissism can be healed only if the offender is crushed and thus the insult to one's narcissism is undone. Revenge, individual and national, is often based on wounded narcissism and on the need to "cure" the wound by the annihilation of the offender.

One last element of narcissistic pathology must be added. The highly narcissistic group is eager to have a leader with whom it can identify itself. The leader is then admired by the group which projects its narcissism onto him. In the very act of submission to the powerful leader, which is in depth an act of symbiosis and identification, the narcissism of the individual is transferred onto the leader. The greater the leader, the greater the follower. Personalities who as individuals are particularly narcissistic are the most qualified to fulfill this function. The narcissism of the leader who is convinced of his greatness, and who has no doubts, is precisely what attracts the narcissism of those who submit to him. The half-insane leader is often the most successful one until his lack of objective judgment, his rage reactions in consequence of any set-back, his need to keep up the image of omnipotence may provoke him to make mistakes which lead to his destruction. But there are always gifted half-psychotics at hand to satisfy the demands of a narcissistic mass.

We have so far discussed the phenomenon of narcissism, its pathology, and its biological and sociological function. As a result we might come to the conclusion that narcissism is a necessary and valuable orientation, provided it is benign and does not transcend a certain threshold. However, our picture is incomplete. Man is not only concerned with biological and social survival, he is also concerned with *values,* with the development of that by virtue of which he is human.

Looking at it from the standpoint of values it becomes evident that narcissism conflicts with reason and with love. This statement hardly needs further elaboration. By the very nature of the narcissistic orientation, it prevents one—to the extent to which it exists—from seeing reality as it is, that is, objectively; in other words, it restricts reason. It may not be equally clear that it restricts love—especially when we recall that Freud said that in all love there is a strong narcissistic component; that a man in love with a woman makes her the object of his own narcissism, and that therefore she becomes wonderful and desirable because she is part of him. She may do the same with him, and thus we have the case of the "great love," which often is only a *folie à deux* rather than love. Both people retain their narcissism, they have no real, deep interest in each other (not to speak of anyone else), they remain touchy and suspicious, and most likely each of them will be in need of a new person who can give them fresh narcissistic satisfaction. For the narcissistic person, the partner is never a person in his own right or in his full reality; he exists only as a shadow of the partner's narcissistically inflated ego. Nonpathological love, on the other hand, is not based on mutual narcissism. It is a relationship between two people who experience themselves as separate entities, yet who can open themselves to and become one with each other. In order to experience love one must experience separateness.

The significance of the phenomenon of narcissism from the ethical-spiritual viewpoint becomes very clear if we consider that the essential teachings of all the great humanist religions can be summarized in one sentence: *It is the goal of man to overcome one's narcissism.* Perhaps this principle is nowhere expressed more radically than in Buddhism. The teaching of the Buddha amounts to saying that man can save himself from suffering only if he awakens from his illusions and becomes aware of his reality; the reality of sickness, old age, and death, and of the impossibility of ever attaining the aims of his greed. The "awakened" person of whom Buddhist teaching speaks is the person who has overcome his narcissism, and who is therefore capable of being fully awake. We might put the same thought still differently: Only if man can do away with the illusion of his indestructible ego, only if he can drop it together with all other objects of his greed, only then can he be open to the world and fully related to it. Psychologically this process of becoming fully awake is identical with the replacement of narcissism by relatedness to the world.

In the Hebrew and Christian traditions the same goal is expressed in various terms which also mean the overcoming of narcissism. The Old Testament says: "Love thy neighbor as thyself." Here the demand is to overcome one's narcissism at least to the point where one's neighbor becomes as important as oneself. But the Old Testament goes much further than this in demanding love for the "stranger." (You know the soul of the stranger, for strangers have you been in the land of Egypt.) The stranger is precisely the person who is not part of my clan, my family, my nation; he is not part of the group to which I am narcissistically attached. He is nothing other than human. One discovers the human being in the stranger, as Hermann Cohen has pointed out.[13] In the love for the stranger narcissistic love has vanished. For it means loving another human being in his suchness and his difference from me, and not because he is like me. When the New Testament says "love thine enemy" it expresses the same idea in a more pointed form. If the stranger has become fully human to you, there is also no longer an enemy, because *you* have become truly human. To love the stranger and the enemy is possible only if narcissism has been overcome, if "I am thou."

The fight against idolatry, which is the central issue of prophetic teaching, is at the same time a fight against narcissism. In idolatry one partial faculty of man is absolutized and made into an idol. Man then worships himself in an alienated form. The idol in which he submerges becomes the object of his narcissistic passion. The idea of God, on the contrary, is the negation of narcissism because only God—not man—is omniscient and omnipotent. But while the concept of an indefinable and indescribable God was the negation of idolatry and narcissism, God soon became again an idol; man identified himself with God in a narcissistic manner, and thus in full contradiction to the

[13] H. Cohen, *Die Religion der Vernunft aus den Quellen des Judentums* (Frankfurt-am-Main: F. Kaufman, 1929).

original function of the concept of God, religion became a manifestation of group narcissism.

The full maturity of man is achieved by his complete emergence
from narcissism, both individual and group narcissism. This goal
of mental development which is thus expressed in psychological
terms is essentially the same as that which the great spiritual
leaders of the human race have expressed in religious-spiritual
terms. While the concepts differ, the substance and the experience
referred to in the various concepts are the same.

We live in a historical period characterized by a sharp discrepancy between the intellectual development of man, which has
led to the development of the most destructive armaments, and
his mental-emotional development, which has left him still in a
state of marked narcissism with all its pathological symptoms.
What can be done in order to avoid the catastrophe which can
easily result from this contradiction? Is it at all possible for man
to take a step in the foreseeable future which, in spite of all
religious teachings, he has never been able to take before? Is
narcissism so deeply ingrained in man that he will never overcome his "narcissistic core," as Freud thought? Is there then any
hope that narcissistic madness will not lead to the destruction of
man before he has had a chance to become fully human? No one
can give an answer to these questions. One can only examine what
the optimal possibilities are which may help man to avoid the
catastrophe.

One might begin with what would seem to be the easiest way.
Even without reducing narcissistic energy in each person, the *object* could be changed. If *mankind,* the entire human family, could
become the object of group narcissism instead of one nation, one
race, or one political system being this object, much might be
gained. If the individual could experience himself primarily as a
citizen of the world and if he could feel pride in mankind and in its
achievements, his narcissism would turn toward the human race as
an object, rather than to its conflicting components. If the educational systems of all countries stressed the achievements of the
human race instead of the achievements of an individual nation,
a more convincing and moving case could be made for the pride

in being man. If the feeling which the Greek poet expressed in Antigone's words, "There is nothing more wonderful than man," could become an experience shared by all, certainly a great step forward would have been taken. Furthermore, another element would have to be added: the feature of all benign narcissism, namely, that it refers to an achievement. Not one group, class, religion, but all of mankind must undertake to accomplish tasks which allow everybody to be proud of belonging to this race. Common tasks for all mankind are at hand: the joint fight against disease, against hunger, for the dissemination of knowledge and art through our means of communication among all the peoples of the world. The fact is that in spite of all differences in political and religious ideology, there is no sector of mankind which can afford to exclude itself from these common tasks; for the great achievement of this century is that the belief in the natural or divine causes of human inequality, of the necessity or legitimacy of the exploitation of one man by another, has been defeated to the point of no return. Renaissance humanism, the bourgeois revolutions, the Russian, Chinese, and colonial revolutions—all are based on one common thought: the equality of man. Even if some of these revolutions have led to the violation of human equality within the systems concerned, the historical fact is that the idea of the equality of all men, hence of their freedom and dignity, has conquered the world, and it is unthinkable that mankind could ever return to the concepts which dominated civilized history until only a short time ago.

The image of the human race and of its achievements as the object of benign narcissism could be represented by supranational organizations such as the United Nations; it could even begin to create its own symbols, holidays, and festivals. Not the national holiday, but the "day of man" would become the highest holiday of the year. But it is clear that such a development can occur only inasmuch as many and eventually all nations concur and are willing to reduce their national sovereignty in favor of the sovereignty of mankind; not only in terms of political, but also in terms of emotional, realities. A strengthened United Nations and the reasonable and peaceful solution of group conflicts are the obvious conditions for the possibility that humanity and its common achievements shall become the object of group narcissism.[14]

Such a change in the object of narcissism from single groups to all mankind and its achievements would indeed tend, as pointed out before, to counteract the dangers of national and ideological narcissism. But this is not enough. If we are true to our political and religious ideals, the Christian as well as the socialist ideal of unselfishness and brotherhood, the task is to reduce the degree of narcissism in each individual. Although this will take generations, it is now more possible than ever before because man has the possibility to create the material conditions for a dignified human life for everybody. The development of technique will do away with the need for one group to enslave and to exploit another; it has already made war obsolete as an economically rational action; man will for the first time emerge from his half-animal state to a fully human one, and hence not need narcissistic satisfaction to compensate for his material and cultural poverty.

On the basis of these new conditions man's attempt to overcome narcissism can be greatly helped by the scientific and the humanist orientations. As I have already indicated, we must shift our educational effort from teaching primarily a technical orientation to one that is scientific; that is, toward furthering critical thought, objectivity, acceptance of reality, and a concept of truth which is subject to no fiat and is valid for every conceivable group. If the civilized nations can create a scientific orientation as one fundamental attitude in their young, much will have been gained in the struggle against narcissism. The second factor which leads in the same direction is the teaching

[14] As an example of more specific measures for such an attempt, I want to mention only a few suggestions. History textbooks should be rewritten as textbooks of *world history*, in which the proportions of each nation's life remain true to reality and are not distorted, just as world maps are the same in all countries and do not inflate the size of each respective country. Furthermore, movies could be made which foster pride in the development of the human race, showing how humanity and its achievements are the final integration of many single steps undertaken by various groups.

of humanist philosophy and anthropology. We cannot expect that all philosophical and religious differences would disappear. We could not even want this, since the establishment of one system claiming to be the "orthodox" one might lead to another source of narcissistic regression. But even allowing for all existing differences, there is a common humanist creed and experience. The creed is that each individual carries all of humanity within himself, that the "human condition" is one and the same for all men, in spite of unavoidable differences in intelligence, talents, height, and color. This humanist experience consists in feeling that nothing human is alien to one, that "I am you," that one can understand another human being because both share the same elements of human existence. This humanist experience is fully possible only if we enlarge our sphere of awareness. Our own awareness is usually confined to what the society of which we are members permits us to be aware. Those human experiences which do not fit into this picture are repressed. Hence our consciousness represents mainly our own society and culture, while our unconscious represents the universal man in each of us.[15] The broadening of self-awareness, transcending consciousness and illuminating the sphere of the social unconscious, will enable man to experience in himself all of humanity; he will experience the fact that he is a sinner and a saint, a child and an adult, a sane and an insane person, a man of the past and one of the future—that he carries within himself that which mankind has been and that which it will be.

A true renaissance of our humanist tradition undertaken by all religions, political, and philosophical systems claiming to represent humanism would, I believe, result in considerable progress toward the most important "new frontier" that exists today—man's development into a completely human being.

By presenting all these thoughts I do not mean to imply that teaching *alone* can be the decisive step for the realization of

---

[15] Cf. E. Fromm, *Zen Buddhism and Psychoanalysis* (New York: Harper & Row, 1960); and *Beyond the Chains of Illusion*, "The Credo Series," planned and edited by Ruth Nanda Anshen (New York: Simon and Schuster, 1962; and New York: Pocket Books, 1963).

humanism, as the Renaissance humanists believed. All these teachings will have an impact only if essential social, economic, and political conditions change; a change from bureaucratic industrialism to humanist-socialist industrialism; from centralization to decentralization; from the organization man to a responsible and participating citizen; subordination of national sovereignties to the sovereignty of the human race and its chosen organs; common efforts of the "have" nations in co-operation with the "have-not" nations to build up the economic systems of the latter; universal disarmament and availability of the existing material resources for constructive tasks. Universal disarmament is also necessary for another reason: if one sector of mankind lives in fear of total destruction by another bloc, and the rest live in fear of destruction by both blocs, then, indeed, group narcissism cannot be diminished. Man can be human only in a climate in which he can expect that he and his children will live to see the next year, and many more years to come.

V

Incestuous Ties

In the previous chapters we have dealt with two orientations—necrophilia and narcissism—which in their extreme forms operate against life and growth and in favor of strife, destruction, and death. In this chapter I shall deal with a third orientation, incestuous symbiosis, which in its malignant form leads to results similar to those of the two orientations discussed before.

Again I shall start out from a central concept of Freud's theory, that of the incestuous fixation to mother. Freud believed this concept to be one of the cornerstones of his scientific edifice, and I believe that his discovery of the fixation to mother is, indeed, one of the most far-reaching discoveries in the science of man. But in this area, as in those discussed before, Freud narrowed his discovery and its consequences by being compelled to couch it in terms of his libido theory.

What Freud observed was the extraordinary energy inherent in a child's attachment to mother, an attachment which is seldom entirely overcome by the average person. Freud had observed the resulting impairment of the man's capacity to relate himself to women, the fact that his independence is weakened, and that the conflict between his conscious goals and the repressed incestuous attachment may lead to various neurotic conflicts and symptoms. Freud believed that the force behind the attachment to mother was, in the case of the little boy, the strength of the genital libido which makes him desire his mother sexually and hate his father as a sexual rival. But in view of the greater strength of this rival, the little boy represses his incestuous desires, and identifies himself with the commands and prohibitions of father. Unconsciously, though, his repressed incestuous wishes linger on, even though only in more pathological cases with great intensity.

As far as the little girl is concerned Freud, in 1931, admitted that he had previously underestimated the duration of her attachment to mother. Sometimes it "comprised by far the longer period of the early sexual efflorescence. . . . These facts show that the pre-Oedipal phase in women is more important than we have hitherto supposed." Freud continues, "It seems that we shall have to retract the universality of the dictum that the Oedipus complex is the nucleus of neurosis." However, he adds that if anyone feels reluctant to adopt this correction he need not do so for one can either "extend the contents of the Oepidus complex to include all the child's relations to both parents or one could say that "women reach the normal Oedipus situation only after surmounting a first phase dominated by the negative complex. . . . Our insight into this pre-Oedipus phase in the little girl's development," concludes Freud, "comes to us as a surprise, comparable in another field with the effect of the discovery of the Minoan-Mycenaean civilization behind that of Greece."[1]

In this last sentence Freud recognized, more implicitly than explicitly, that the attachment to mother is common to both sexes as the earliest phase of development and that it can be compared with the matriarchal features of pre-Hellenic culture. But he did not follow up this thought. First of all, he concluded, somewhat paradoxically, that the phase of Oedipal attachment to the mother, which may be called the pre-Oedipus phase, is far more important in women than it can claim to be in men.[2] Second, he understands this pre-Oedipus phase of the little girl only in terms of the libido theory. He comes near to transcending it when he remarks that the complaint of many women of not having suckled long enough leaves him in doubt "if one analysed

[1] S. Freud, *Collected Papers*, Vol. V, pp. 253-54.
[2] *Ibid.*, p. 258.

children who had been suckled as long as in primitive races, one would not encounter the same complaint." But his answer is only: "so great is the greed of the childish libido."[3, 4]

This pre-Oedipal attachment of boys and girls to their mother, which is qualitatively different from the Oedipal attachment of boys to their mother is in my experience by far the more important phenomenon, in comparison with which the genital incestuous desires of the little boy are quite secondary. I find that the boy's or girl's pre-Oedipus attachment to mother is one of the central phenomena in the evolutionary process and one of the main causes of neurosis or psychosis. Rather than call it a manifestation of the libido, I would prefer to describe its quality which, whether we use the term libido or not, is something entirely different from the boy's genital desires. This 'incestuous' striving, in the pre-genital sense, is one of the most fundamental passions in men or women, comprising the human being's desire for protection, the satisfaction of his narcissism; his craving to be freed from the risks of responsibility, of freedom, of awareness; his longing for unconditional love, which is offered without any expectation of his loving response. It is true these needs exist normally in the infant, and the mother is the person who fulfills them. The infant could not live if this were not so; it is helpless, cannot depend on its own resources, needs love and care which do not depend on any merits of its own. If it is not mother who fulfills this function, it is another "mothering person," as H. S. Sullivan called her, who can undertake the mother's function; maybe a grandmother or an aunt.

But the more obvious fact—that the infant needs a mothering person—has obscured the fact that not only the infant is helpless and craves certainty; the adult is in many ways not less helpless. Indeed, he can work and fulfill the tasks ascribed to him by society; but he is also more aware than the infant of the dangers and risks of life; he knows of the natural and social forces he cannot control, the accidents he cannot foresee, the sickness and

[3] *Ibid.*, p. 262.
[4] Freud explicitly argues against Melanie Klein's theory that the Oedipus complex begins as early as the second year of a child's life (*op. cit.*, p. 270).

death he cannot elude. What could be more natural, under the circumstances, than man's frantic longing for a power which gives him certainty, protection, and love? This desire is not only a "repetition" of his longing for mother; it is generated because the very same conditions which make the infant long for mother's love continue to exist, although on a different level. If human beings—men and women—could find "Mother" for the rest of their lives, life would be relieved of its risks and of its tragedy. Should we be surprised that man is driven so relentlessly to pursue this *fata morgana*?

Yet man also knows more or less clearly that the lost paradise cannot be found; that he is condemned to live with uncertainty and risks; that he has to rely on his own efforts, and that only the full development of his powers can give him a modicum of strength and fearlessness. Thus he is torn between two tendencies since the moment of his birth: one, to emerge to the light and the other to regress to the womb; one for adventure and the other for certainty; one for the risk of independence and the other for protection and dependence.

Genetically, mother is the first personification of the power that protects and guarantees certainty. But she is by no means the only one. Later on, when the child grows up, mother as a person is often replaced or complemented by the family, the clan, by all who share the same blood and have been born on the same soil. Later, when the size of the group increases, the race and the nation, religion or political parties become the "mothers," the guarantors of protection and love. In more archaically oriented persons, nature herself, the earth and the sea, become the great representatives of the "mother." The transference of the motherly function from the real mother to the family, the clan, the nation, the race has the same advantage which we have already noted with regard to the transformation from personal to group narcissism. First of all, anybody's mother is likely to die before her children; hence the need for a mother figure which is immortal. Furthermore, the allegiance to one personal mother leaves one alone and isolated from others who have different mothers. If, however, the whole clan, the nation, the race, the religion, or God can become a common "mother," then mother-worship transcends the individual and unites him with all those who worship the same mother idol; then nobody needs to be embarrassed at idolizing his mother; the praise of the "mother" common to the group will unite all minds and eliminate all jealousies. The many cults of the Great Mother, the cult of the Virgin, the cult of nationalism and patriotism—they all bear witness to the intensity of this worship. Empirically the fact can easily be established that there is a close correlation between persons with a strong fixation to their mothers and those with exceptionally strong ties to nation and race, soil and blood.[5]

A word needs to be added here concerning the role of the sexual factor in the tie to mother. For Freud the sexual factor was the decisive element in the little boy's attraction to mother. Freud came to this result by combining two facts: the boy's attraction to mother, and the fact of the existence of his genital striving at an early age. Freud explained the first fact by the second. There is no doubt that in many cases the little boy has sexual desires for his mother, and the little girl for her father; but quite aside from the fact (which Freud at first saw, then denied, and which was taken up again by Ferenczi) that the seductive influence of the parents is a very important cause for these incestuous strivings, the sexual strivings are not the cause of the fixation to mother, but the *result*. Furthermore, in incestual sexual desires which one finds in the dreams of adults, it can be established that the sexual desire is often a defense against a deeper regression; by asserting his male sexuality, the man defends himself against his own desire to return to the mother's breast or into her womb.

Another aspect of the same problem is the incestuous fixation of daughters to their mothers. While in the boy the fixation to "mother" in the broad sense used here coincides with whatever sexual elements may enter into the relationship, with girls this

---

[5] It is interesting to note in this context that the Sicilian Mafia, a closely bound secret society of men, from which women are excluded (and by which, incidentally, they are never harmed) is called "Mama" by its members.

is not so. Her sexual attraction would be directed toward the father, while the incestuous fixation, in our sense, would be directed toward mother. This very split makes it more clear that even the deepest incestuous bond with mother can exist without a trace of sexual stimulation. There is a great deal of clinical experience with women who have as intense an incesuous tie with mother as can be found in man.

The incestuous tie to mother very frequently implies not only a longing for mother's love and protection, but also a fear of her. This fear is first of all the result of the very dependency which weakens the person's own sense of strength and independence; it can also be the fear of the very tendencies which we find in the case of deep regression: that of being the suckling or of returning to mother's womb. These very wishes transform the mother into a dangerous cannibal, or an all-destroying monster. It must be added, however, that very frequently such fears are not primarily the result of a person's regressive fantasies, but are caused by the fact that the mother is in reality a cannibalistic, vampirelike, or necrophilic person. If a son or a daughter of such a mother grows up without breaking the ties to her, then he or she cannot escape from suffering intense fears of being eaten up or destroyed by mother. The only course which in such cases can cure the fears that may drive a person to the border of insanity is the capacity to cut the tie with mother. But the fear which is engendered in such a relationship is at the same time the reason why it is so difficult for a person to cut the umbilical cord. Inasmuch as a person remains caught in this dependency, his own independence, freedom, and responsibility are weakened.[6]

So far I have tried to give a general picture of the nature of the irrational dependence and fear of mother as distinguished from the sexual ties in which Freud saw the nucleus of incestuous strivings. But there is another aspect to the problem, as in the

---

[6] In some important aspects my views are similar to those of Jung, who was the first to liberate the incest complex from its narrow sexual confines. In many essential points I differ from Jung, but it would burden this short volume too much if I went into a discourse of these differences.

other phenomena which we have discussed so far, namely the *degree of regression* within the incestuous complex. Here too, we can distinguish between very benign forms of "mother fixation," forms which in fact are so benign that they can hardly be called pathological, and malignant forms of incestuous fixation which I call "incestuous symbiosis."

On the benign level we find a form of mother fixation which is rather frequent. Such men need a woman to comfort them, love them, admire them; they want to be mothered, fed, cared for. If they fail to obtain this kind of love they tend to feel slightly anxious and depressed. When this mother fixation is of slight intensity it will not impair the man's sexual or affective potency, or his independence and integrity. It may even be surmised that in most men there remains an element of such fixation and the desire to find something of the mother in a woman. If, however, the intensity of this tie is greater, one usually finds certain conflicts and symptoms of a sexual or emotional nature.

There is a second level of incestuous fixation which is much more serious and neurotic. (In speaking of distinct levels here, I am only choosing a form of description which is convenient for the purpose of a brief presentation; in reality there are not three distinct levels; there is a continuum which stretches from the most harmless to the most malignant forms of incestuous fixation. The levels I describe here are typical points in this continuum; in a more fully developed discussion of this topic, each level could be divided into at least several "sublevels.") On this level of mother fixation the person has failed to develop his independence. In its less severe forms it is a fixation which makes it necessary always to have a mothering figure at hand, waiting, making few or no demands, the person on whom one can depend unconditionally. In its more severe manifestations we might find a man, for instance, who chooses a wife who is a stern mother-figure; he feels like a prisoner who has no right to do anything which is not in the service of the wife-mother, and he is constantly afraid of her, lest she might be angry. He will probably rebel unconsciously, then feel guilty and submit all the more obediently. The rebellion may manifest itself in sexual infidelity, depressive moods, sudden outbursts of anger, psychosomatic symptoms, or general obstructionism. This man may also suffer from serious doubts in his manliness, or from sexual disturbances such as impotence or homosexuality.

Different from this picture in which anxiety and rebellion dominate, is another where mother fixation is mixed with a seductive male-narcissistic attitude. Often such men at an early age felt that mother preferred them to father; that they were admired by mother, while the father was held in contempt. They develop a strong narcissism which makes them feel that they are better than father—or rather, better than any other man. This narcissistic conviction makes it unnecessary for them to do much, or anything, to prove their greatness. Their greatness is built on the tie to mother. Consequently, for such men their whole sense of self-worth is bound up with the relationship to the women who admire them unconditionally and without limits. Their greatest fear is that they may fail to obtain the admiration of a woman they have chosen, since such failure would threaten the basis of their narcissistic self-evaluation. But while they are afraid of women, this fear is less obvious than in the previous case, because the picture is dominated by their narcissistic-seductive attitude that gives the impression of warm manliness. However, in this, as in any other type of intense mother fixation, it is a crime to feel love, interest, loyalty toward anyone, whether men or women, except the mother figure. One must not even be *interested* in anybody or anything else, including work, because mother demands exclusive allegiance. Often such men have a guilty conscience if they have even a most harmless interest in anything, or they develop into the type of "traitor" who cannot be loyal to anybody, because they cannot be disloyal to mother.

Here are some dreams characteristic of mother fixation.

    1. A man dreams that he is alone on the beach. An elderly woman comes and smiles at him. She indicates to him that he may drink from her breast.

2. A man dreams that a powerful woman has seized him, holds him over a deep ravine, drops him, and he falls to his death.

3. A woman dreams that she is meeting a man; at that moment a witch appears and the dreamer is deeply frightened. The man takes a gun and kills the witch. She (the dreamer) runs away, being afraid of being discovered, and beckons to the man to follow her.

These dreams hardly need explanation. In the first one the main element is the wish to be nursed by mother; in the second, the fear of being destroyed by an all-powerful mother; in the third, the woman dreams that her mother (the witch) will destroy her if she falls in love with a man, and only her mother's death can liberate her.

But what about fixation to father? Indeed, there is no doubt that such fixation exists both among men and among women; in the latter case it sometimes is blended with sexual desires. Yet it seems that fixation to father never reaches the depth of fixation to mother-family-blood-earth. While of course in some particular case father himself can be a mothering figure, normally his function is different from mother's. It is she who in the first years of life nurses the child and gives it that feeling of being protected which is part of the mother-fixated person's eternal desire. The infant's life depends on mother—hence she can give life and take away life. The mother figure is at the same time that of the life-giver and that of the life-destroyer, the loved one and the feared one.[7] The father's function, on the other hand, is a different one. He represents man-made law and order, social rules and duties, and he is the one who punishes or rewards. His love is conditional, and can be won by doing what is required. For this reason the person bound to father can more easily hope to gain his love by doing father's will; but the euphoric feeling of complete and unconditional love, certainty and protec-

[7] Cf. in mythology, for instance, the double role of the Indian goddess Kali, and in dreams the symbolization of mother as a tiger, lion, witch or child-eating sorceress.

tion is rarely present in the experience of the father-bound person.[8] We also rarely find in the father-centered person the depth of regression which we are now going to describe with regard to mother fixation.

The deepest level of mother fixation is that of "incestuous symbiosis." What is meant by "symbiosis"? There are various degrees of symbiosis, but they all have in common one element: the symbiotically attached person is part and parcel of the "host" person to whom he is attached. He cannot live without that person, and if the relationship is threatened he feels extremely anxious and frightened. (In patients close to schizophrenia the separation may lead to a sudden schizophrenic breakdown.) When I say he cannot live without that person I do not mean that he is necessarily always physically together with the host person; he may see him or her only rarely, or the host person may even be dead (in this case the symbiosis may take the form of what in some cultures is institutionalized as "ancestor worship"); the bond is essentially one of feeling and fantasy. For the symbiotically attached person it is very difficult, if not impossible, to sense a clear delineation between himself and the host person. He feels himself to be one with the other, a part of her, blended with her. The more extreme the form of symbiosis, the less possible is a clear realization of the separateness of the two persons. This lack of separateness explains also why in the more severe cases it would be misleading to speak of a "dependency" of the symbiotically attached person to his host. "Dependency" presupposes the clear distinction between two persons, one of whom is dependent on the other. In the case of a symbiotic relationship the symbiotically attached person may sometimes feel superior, sometimes inferior, sometimes equal to the host person—but always they are inseparable. Actually, this symbiotic unity can best be exemplified by mentioning the unity of the mother with the fetus. Fetus and

[8] I will mention only in passing the difference in structure between mother-centered and father-centered cultures and religions. The Catholic countries in the south of Europe and Latin America and the Protestant countries in northern Europe and North America are good examples. The psychological differences have been dealt with by Max Weber in *Protestant Ethic* and by myself in *Escape from Freedom*.

mother are two, and yet they are one.[9] It happens also, and not too rarely, that both persons involved are symbiotically attached, each to the other. In this case one is dealing with a *folie à deux*, which makes the two unaware of their *folie* because their shared system constitutes reality for them. In the extremely regressive forms of symbiosis the unconscious desire is actually that of returning to the womb. Often this wish is expressed in symbolic form as the wish (or fear) of being drowned in the ocean, or the fear of being swallowed by the earth; it is a desire to lose completely one's individuality, to become one again with nature. It follows that this deep regressive desire conflicts with the wish to live. To be in the womb is to be removed from life.

What I have been trying to say is that the tie to mother, both the wish for her love and the fear of her destructiveness, is much stronger and more elementary than Freud's "Oedipus tie," which he thought was based on sexual desires. There is a problem, however, which lies in the discrepancy between our conscious perception and the unconscious reality. If a man remembers or imagines sexual desires toward his mother, he meets with the difficulty of resistance, yet since the nature of sexual desire is known to him, it is only the *object* of his desire of which his consciousness does not want to be aware. It is quite different with the symbiotic fixation we are discussing here, the wish of being loved like an infant, losing all one's independence, being a suckling again, or even being in mother's womb; all these are desires which are by no means covered by the words "love," "dependence," or even "sexual fixation." All these words are pallid in comparison with the power of the experience behind them. The same holds true of the "fear of mother." We all know what it means to be afraid of a person. He may scold us, humiliate us, punish us. We have gone through this experience and faced it with more or less courage. But do we know how we would feel if we were to be pushed into a cage where a lion expected us, or if we were thrown into a pit filled with snakes? Can we express the terror which would strike us, seeing ourselves sentenced to

[9] Cf. M. A. Lechehaye's *Symbolic Realization*, International Universities Press, 1955, an excellent description of the symbiotic fixation of a severely disturbed patient.

trembling impotence? Yet it is precisely this kind of experience which constitutes the "fear" of mother. The words we use here make it very difficult to reach the unconscious experience, and hence people often speak of their dependence, or fear, without really knowing what they are talking about. The language which is adequate to describe the real experience is that of dreams or symbols in mythology and religion. If I dream that I am drowning in the ocean (accompanied by a feeling of mixed dread and bliss), or if I dream that I am trying to escape from a lion that is about to swallow me, then indeed, I dream in a language which corresponds to what I really experience. Our everyday language corresponds, of course, to the experiences which we permit ourselves to be aware of. If we want to penetrate to our inner reality we must try to forget customary language and think in the forgotten language of symbolism.

The pathology of incestuous fixation depends obviously on the level of regression. In the most benign cases there is hardly any pathology to speak of except, perhaps, a slight overdependence on and fear of women. The deeper the level of regression the more intense are both the dependence and the fear. On the most archaic level, both dependence and fear have reached a degree which conflicts with sane living. There are other elements of pathology which also depend on the depth of regression. The incestuous orientation conflicts, as narcissism does, with reason and objectivity. If I fail to cut the umbilical cord, if I insist on worshiping the idol of certainty and protection, then the idol becomes sacred. It must not be criticized. If "mother" cannot be wrong, how can I judge anyone else objectively if he is in conflict with "mother" or disapproved of by her? This form of impairment of judgment is much less obvious when the object of fixation is not mother but the family, the nation, or the race. Since these fixations are supposed to be virtues, a strong national or religious fixation easily leads to biased and distorted judgments which are taken for truth because they are shared by all others who participate in the same fixation.

After the distortion of reason, the second most important pathological trait in incestuous fixation is the lack of experiencing another being as fully human. Only those who share the same blood or soil are felt to be human; the "stranger" is a barbarian. As a consequence I remain also a "stranger" to myself, since I cannot experience humanity beyond that crippled form in which it is shared by the group united by common blood. Incestuous fixation impairs or destroys—in accordance with the degree of regression—the capacity to love.

The third pathological symptom of incestuous fixation is conflict with independence and integrity. The person bound to mother and tribe is not free to be himself, to have a conviction of his own, to be committed. He cannot be open to the world, nor can he embrace it; he is always in the prison of the motherly racial-national-religious fixation. Man is only fully born, and thus free to move forward and to become himself, to the degree to which he liberates himself from all forms of incestuous fixation.

Incestuous fixation is usually not recognized as such, or it is rationalized in such a way as to make it appear reasonable. Somebody strongly bound to his mother may rationalize his incestuous tie in various ways: It is my duty to serve her; or, She did so much for me and I owe her my life; or, She has suffered so much; or, She is so wonderful. If the object of fixation is not the individual mother but the nation, the rationalizations are similar. In the center of the rationalizations is the concept that one owes everything to the nation, or that the nation is so extraordinary and so wonderful.

To sum up: The tendency to remain bound to the mothering person and her equivalents—to blood, family, tribe—is inherent in all men and women. It is constantly in conflict with the opposite tendency—to be born, to progress, to grow. In the case of normal development, the tendency for growth wins. In the case of severe pathology, the regressive tendency for symbiotic union wins, and it results in the person's more or less total incapacitation. Freud's concept of the incestuous strivings to be found in any child is perfectly correct. Yet the significance of this concept transcends Freud's own assumption. Incestuous wishes are not primarily a result of sexual desires, but constitute one of the most fundamental tendencies in man: the wish to remain tied to where he came from, the fear of being free, and the fear of being destroyed by the very figure toward whom he has made himself helpless, renouncing any independence.

We are now in a position to compare the three tendencies this book has dealt with in their relationship to each other. In their less severe manifestations, necrophilia, narcissism, and incestuous fixation are quite different from each other, and very often a person may have one of these orientations without sharing in the others. Also, in their nonmalignant forms no one of these orientations causes grave incapacitation of reason and love, or creates intense destructiveness. (As an example for this I would like to mention the person of Franklin D. Roosevelt. He was moderately mother-fixed, moderately narcissistic, and a strongly biophilous person. In contrast Hitler was an almost totally necrophilous, narcissistic and incestuous person). But the more malignant the three orientations are, the more they converge. First of all there is a close affinity between incestuous fixation and narcissism. Inasmuch as the individual has not yet fully emerged from mother's womb or mother's breasts, he is not free to relate to others or to love others. He and his mother (as one) are the object of his narcissism. This can be seen most clearly where the personal narcissism has been transformed into group narcissism. There we find very clearly incestuous fixation blended with narcissism. It is this particular blend which explains the power and the irrationality of all national, racial, religious and political fanaticism.

In the most archaic forms of incestuous symbiosis and narcissism they are joined by necrophilia. The craving to return to the womb and to the past is at the same time the craving for death and destruction. If extreme forms of necrophilia, narcissism, and incestuous symbiosis are blended, we can speak of a syndrome which I propose to call the "syndrome of decay." The person suffering from this syndrome is indeed evil, since he betrays life and growth and is a devotee of death and crippledness. The best-documented example of a man suffering from the "syndrome of decay" is Hitler. He was, as I indicated before, deeply attracted to death and destruction; he was an extremely narcissistic person for whom the only reality was *his own* wishes and thoughts. Finally, he was an extremely incestuous person. Whatever his relationship to his mother may have been, his incestuousness was mainly expressed in his fanatical devotion to the race, the people who shared the same blood. He was obsessed by the idea of saving the Germanic race by preventing its blood from being poisoned. First of all, as he expressed it in *Mein Kampf,* to save it from syphilis; second, to save it from being polluted by Jews. Narcissism, death, and incest were the fatal blend which made a man like Hitler one of the enemies of mankind and of life. This triade of traits has been most succinctly described by Richard Hughes in *The Fox in the Attic*:

After all, how could that monistic "I" of Hitler's ever without forfeit succumb to the entire act of sex, the whole essence of which is recognition of one "Other"? Without damage I mean to his fixed conviction that he was the universe's unique sentient centre, the sole authentic incarnate Will it contained or had ever contained? Because this of course was the rationale of his supernal inner "Power": *Hitler existed alone.* "I am, none else beside me." The universe contained no other persons than him, only things; and thus for him the whole gamut of the "personal" pronouns lacked wholly its normal emotional content. This left Hitler's designing and creating motions enormous and without curb: it was only natural for this architect to turn also politician for he saw no real distinction in the new things to be handled: these "men" were merely him-mimicking "things," in the same category as other tools and stones. All tools have handles—this sort was fitted with ears. And it is nonsensical to love or hate or pity (or tell the truth to) stones.

Hitler's then was that rare diseased state of the personality, an ego virtually without penumbra: rare and diseased, that is, when abnormally such an ego survives in an otherwise mature adult intelligence clinically sane (for in the new-born doubtless it is a beginning normal enough and even surviving into the young child). Hitler's *adult* "I" had developed thus—into a larger but still undifferentiated structure, as a malignant growth does. . . .

The tortured, demented creature tossed on his bed. . . .

"Rienzi-night," that night on the Freinberg over Linz after the opera: that surely had been the climactic night of his boyhood for it was then he had first confirmed that lonely omnipotence within him. Impelled to go up there in the darkness into that high place had he not been shown there all earthly kingdoms in a moment of time? And facing there the ancient gospel question had not his whole being been one assenting Yea? Had he not *struck* the everlasting bargain there on the high mountain under the witnessing November stars? Yet now . . . now, when he had seemed to be riding Rienzi-like the crest of the wave, the irresistible wave which with mounting force should have carried him to Berlin, that crest had begun to curl: it had curled and broken and toppled on him, thrusting him down, down in the green thundering water, deep.

Tossing desperately on his bed, he gasped—he was drowning (what of all things always Hitler most feared). *Drowning?* Then . . . that suicidal boyhood moment's teetering long ago on the Danube bridge at Linz . . . after all the melancholic boy *had* leaped that long-ago day, and everything since was dream! Then this noise now was the mighty Danube singing in his dreaming drowning ears.

In the green watery light surrounding him a dead face was floating towards him upturned: a dead face with his own slightly-bulging eyes in it unclosed: his dead Mother's face as he had last seen it with unclosed eyes white on the white pillow. Dead, and white, and vacant even of its love for him.

But now that face was multiplied—it was all around him in the water. So his Mother *was* this water, these waters drowning him!

At that he ceased to struggle. He drew up his knees to his chin in the primal attitude and lay there, letting himself drown.

So Hitler slept at last.[10]

In this short passage all the elements of the "syndrome of decay" have been brought together in the way only a great writer can do. We see Hitler's narcissism, his longing to drown—the water being his mother—and his affinity to death, symbolized by his dead mother's face. The regression to the womb is symbolized in his posture, with his knees drawn up to his chin in the primal attitude.

Hitler is only one outstanding example of the "syndrome of decay." There are many who thrive on violence, hate, racism, and narcissistic nationalism, and who suffer from this syndrome. They are the leaders of or the "true believers" in violence, war, and destruction. Only the most unbalanced and sick among them will express their true aims explicitly, or even be aware of them consciously. They will tend to rationalize their orientation as love of country, duty, honor, etc. But when the forms of normal

---

[10] Richard Hughes, *The Fox in the Attic* (New York: Harper & Row, 1961), pp. 266-68.

civilized life have broken down, as happens in international war or civil war, such people no longer need to repress their deepest desires; they will sing hymns of hate; they will come to life and unfold all their energies at times when they can serve death. Indeed, war and an atmosphere of violence is the situation in which the person with the "syndrome of decay" becomes fully himself. Most likely it is only a minority of the population who are motivated by this syndrome. Yet the very fact that neither they nor those who are not so motivated are aware of the real motivation makes them dangerous carriers of an infectious disease, a hate infection, in times of strife, conflict, cold and hot war. Hence it is important that they be recognized for what they are: men who love death, who are afraid of independence, for whom only the needs of their own group have reality. They would not have to be isolated physically, as is done with lepers; it would be sufficient if persons who are normal were to understand their crippledness and the malignancy of the strivings hidden behind their pious rationalizations, in order that normal persons might acquire a certain degree of immunity to their pathological influence. In order to do this it is, of course, necessary to learn one thing: not to take words for reality, and to see through the deceptive rationalizations of those who suffer from a sickness that only man is capable of suffering from: the negation of life before life has vanished.[11]

Our analysis of necrophilia, narcissism, and incestuous fixation suggests a discussion of the point of view presented here in relation to Freudian theory, even though this discussion must necessarily be brief in the context of this book.

Freud's thinking was based on an evolutionary scheme of libido development, from the narcissistic to the oral-receptive, oral-

---

[11] I suggest an empirical program of research which would permit discovering, by means of a "projective questionnaire," the incidence of people suffering from necrophilia, extreme narcissism, and incestuous symbiosis; such a questionnaire could be applied to a stratified and representative sample of the United States population. This would make it possible not only to discover the incidence of the "syndrome of decay" but also its relation to other factors, such as socio-economic position, education, religion, and geographical origin.

aggressive, anal-sadistic, to the phallic- and genital-character orientations. According to Freud the gravest type of mental sickness was that caused by a fixation on (or regression to) the earliest levels of development of the libido. As a consequence, for example, regression to the oral-receptive level would be considered a more severe pathology than regression to the anal-sadistic level. In my experience, however, this general princinple is not born out by clinically observable facts. The oral-receptive orientation is in itself one that is closer to life than is the anal orientation; hence, generally speaking, the anal orientation could be said to be conducive to more severe pathology than the oral-receptive. Furthermore, the oral-aggressive orientation would seem to be more conducive to severe pathology than the oral-receptive, because of the element of sadism and destructiveness involved in it. As a result, we would arrive almost at a reversal of the Freudian scheme. The least severe pathology would be that connected with the oral-receptive orientation, followed by more severe pathology in the oral-aggressive and in the anal-sadistic orientations. Assuming the validity of Freud's observation that genetically the sequence of development is from the oral-receptive to the oral-aggressive to the anal-sadistic orientation, one would have to disagree with his standpoint that fixation on an earlier phase means more severe pathology.

However, I believe that the problem cannot be solved by the evolutionary assumption that the earlier orientations are the roots for the more pathological manifestations. As I see it, each orientation in itself has various levels of regression, reaching from normal to the most archaic pathological level. The oral-receptive orientation, for instance, can be mild when it is combined with a generally mature character structure, that is, a high degree of productivity. On the other hand, it can be combined with a high degree of narcissism and incestuous symbiosis; in this case the oral-receptive orientation will be one of extreme dependency and malignant pathology. The same holds true as regards the almost normal anal character in comparison with the necrophilic character. I propose therefore to determine pathology not according to the distinction between the various levels in libido development, but according to the degree of regression which can be determined *within* each orientation (oral-receptive, oral-aggressive, etc.) It must furthermore be kept in mind that we are dealing not only with the orientation which Freud sees as being rooted in the respective erogenous zones (modes of assimilation), but also with forms of personal related-ness (like love, destructiveness, sado-masochism) which have certain affinities to the various modes of assimilation.[12] Thus, for instance, there is an affinity between the oral-receptive and the incestuous, between the anal and the destructive orientations. In this book I am dealing with orientations in the realm of relatedness (narcissism, necrophilia, incestuous orientation—"modes of socialization") rather than with the modes of assimilation; but there is a correlation between the two modes of orientation. In the case of the affinity between necrophilia and the anal orientation this correlation has been demonstrated in some de-tail in this book. It exists also between biophilia and the "genital character" and between incestuous fixation and the oral char-acter.

I have tried to show that each of the three orientations described here can occur on various levels of regression. The deeper the regression in each orientation, the more the three tend to converge. In the state of extreme regression they have con-verged to form what I have called the "syndrome of decay." On the other hand, with the person who has reached an optimum of maturity, the three orientations also tend to converge. The op-posite of necrophilia is biophilia; the opposite of narcissism is love; the opposite of incestuous symbiosis is independence and freedom. The syndrome of these three attitudes I call the "syndrome of growth." The following figure shows this concept in schematic form.

[12] Cf. E. Fromm, *Man for Himself*, pp. 62 ff.

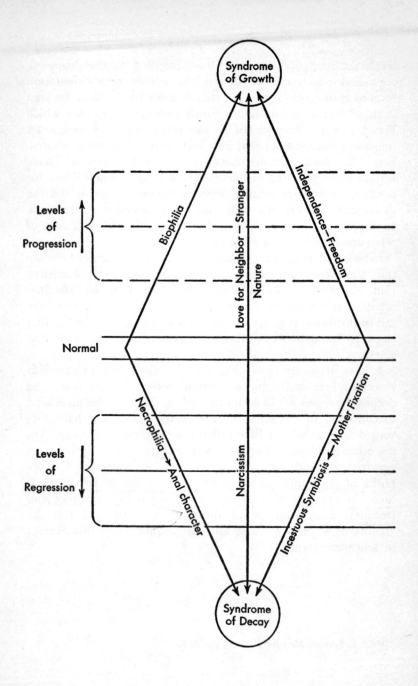

VI
Freedom, Determinism, Alternativism

Having discussed some of the empirical problems of destructiveness and violence we are now perhaps better prepared to take up the threads that were left loose in Chapter 1. Let us return to the question: Is man good or evil? Is he free or is he determined by circumstances? Or are these alternatives wrong and is man neither this nor that—or is he both this and that?

To answer these questions it will serve our purpose best if we begin with the discussion of still another question. Can one speak of the essence or nature of man, and if so, how can it be defined?

As to the question whether one can speak of an essence of man, one readily finds two contradictory viewpoints: One says that there is no such thing as an *essence* of man; this viewpoint is held by anthropological relativism, which claims that man is nothing but the product of cultural patterns which mold him. On the other hand, the empirical discussion on destructiveness in this book is rooted in the view held by Freud and many others that there is such a thing as the nature of man; in fact, all dynamic psychology is based on this premise.

The difficulty in finding a satisfactory definition for the nature of man lies in the following dilemma: If one assumes a certain *substance* as constituting the essence of man, one is forced into a nonevolutionary, unhistorical position which implies that there has been no basic change in man since the very beginning of his emergence. Such a view is difficult to square with the fact that there is a tremendous difference to be found between our most undeveloped ancestors and civilized man as he appears in the last four to six thousand years of history.[1] On the other hand, if one accepts an evolutionary concept and thus believes that man is constantly changing, what is left as a content for an alleged "nature" or "essence" of man? This dilemma is also not solved by such "definitions" of man as that he is a political animal (Aristotle), an animal that can promise (Nietzsche), or an animal that produces with foresight and imagination (Marx); these definitions express *essential qualities* of man, but they do not refer to *the essence* of man.

I believe that the dilemma can be solved by defining the essence of man not as a given quality or substance, but as a *contradiction inherent in human existence*.[2] This contradiction is to be found in two sets of facts: (1) Man is an animal, yet his instinctual equipment, in comparison with that of all other animals, is incomplete and not sufficient to ensure his survival unless he produces the means to satisfy his material needs and develops speech and tools. (2) Man has intelligence, like other animals, which permits him to use thought processes for the attainment of immediate, practical aims; but man has another mental quality which the animal lacks. He is aware of himself, of his past and of his future, which is death; of his smallness and powerlessness; he is aware of

---

[1] Marx was particularly bothered by this dilemma. He spoke of the "essence of man" although after the Economic and Philosophical manuscripts of 1844 he stopped using this expression and spoke, for instance, of the "uncrippled" man, which presupposes the concept of a nature of man which can be crippled. (In *Capital*, Vol. III he still used the concept of 'human nature', speaking of unalienated work as one under conditions "most adequate to their human nature and most worthy of it.") On the other hand, Marx stressed that man creates himself in the process of history, and at one point he even went so far as to stress that the essence of man is nothing but the social ensemble" in which he lives. It is quite evident that Marx did not want to give up the concept of a nature of man, yet that he did not want to surrender to an unhistorical, nonevolutionary concept either. The fact is that Marx never solved the dilemma, and hence did not arrive at a definition of the nature of man, and so his utterances on this subject remained somewhat vague and contradictory.

[2] I have expressed the ideas presented in the next few pages in *The Sane Society* (New York: Holt, Rinehart and Winston, 1955). I have to repeat them here in a condensed form because otherwise the main part of this chapter would be lacking a basis.

others as others—as friends, enemies, or as strangers. Man transcends all other life because he is, for the first time, *life aware of itself*. Man is *in* nature, subject to its dictates and accidents, yet he *transcends* nature because he lacks the unawareness which makes the animal a part of nature—as one with it. Man is confronted with the frightening conflict of being the prisoner of nature, yet being free in his thoughts; being a part of nature, and yet to be as it were a freak of nature; being neither here nor there. Human self-awareness has made man a stranger in the world, separate, lonely, and frightened.

The contradiction I have described so far is essentially the same as the classic view that man is both body and soul, angel and animal, that he belongs to two worlds in conflict with each other. What I want to point out now is that it is not enough to see this conflict as the essence of man, that is to say, as that by virtue of which man is man. It is necessary to go beyond this description and to recognize that the very conflict in man *demands a solution*. Certain questions arise immediately from the statement of the conflict: What can man do to cope with this fright inherent in his existence? What can man do to find a harmony to liberate him from the torture of aloneness, and to permit him to be at home in the world, to find a sense of unity?

The answer man must give to these questions is not a theoretical one (although it is reflected in the ideas and theories about life), but it is one of his whole being, his feeling and acting. The answer may be better or worse, but even the worst answer is better than none. There is one condition which every answer must fulfill: it must help man to overcome the sense of separateness and to gain a sense of union, of oneness, of belonging. There are a number of answers that man can give to the question which the fact of having been born human asks him, and I shall briefly discuss them in the following pages. I want to stress again that none of these answers as such constitutes the essence of man; what constitutes the essence is the question and the need for an answer; the various forms of human existence are not the essence, but they are the answers to the conflict which, in itself, is the essence.

The first answer to the quest to transcend separateness and to achieve unity I call the *regressive* answer. If man wants to find unity, if he wants to be freed from the fright of loneliness and uncertainty, he can try to return to where he came from—to nature, to animal life, or to his ancestors. He can try to do away with that which makes him human and yet tortures him: his reason and self-awareness. It seems that for hundreds of thousands of years man tried just that. The history of primitive religions is a witness to this attempt, and so is severe psychopathology in the individual. In one form or another both in primitive religions and in individual psychology, we find the same severe pathology: regression to animal existence, to the state of pre-individuation, the attempt to do away with that which is specifically human. This statement, however, must be qualified in one sense. If regressive archaic trends are shared by many, we have the picture of a *folie à millions;* the very fact of the consensus makes the folly appear as wisdom, the fiction as real. The individual who participates in this common folly lacks the sense of complete isolation and separation, and hence escapes the intense anxiety he would experience in a progressive society. It must be remembered that for most people reason and reality are nothing but public consensus. One never "loses one's mind" when nobody else's mind differs from one's own.

The alternative to the regressive, archaic solution to the problem of human existence, to the burden of being man, is the *progressive solution,* that of finding a new harmony not by regression but by the full development of all *human* forces, of the humanity within oneself. The progressive solution was visualized for the first time in a radical form (there are many religions which form the transition between the archaic regressive and humanist religions) in that remarkable period of human history between 1500 B.C. and 500 B.C. It appeared in Egypt around 1350 B.C. in the teachings of Ikhnaton, with the Hebrews around the same time in the teachings of Moses; around 600 to 500 B.C. the same idea was announced by Lao-Tse in China, by the Buddha in India, by Zarathustra in Persia, and by the philosophers in Greece as well as by the prophets in Israel. The new goal of man, that of becoming fully human and thus regaining his lost harmony was expressed in different concepts and symbols. For Eknaton the goal was symbolized by the Sun; for Moses by the unknown God of history; Lao-Tse called the goal Tao (the way); Buddha symbolized it as Nirvanah; the Greek philosophers as the unmoved mover; the Persians as Zarathustra; the prophets as the Messianic "end of the days." These concepts were to a large extent determined by the modes of thought, and in the last analysis by the practice of life and the socio-economic-political structure of each of these cultures. But while the particular form in which the new goal was expressed depended on various historical circumstances, the goal was essentially the same: to solve the problem of human existence by giving the right answer to the question which life poses it, that of man's becoming fully human and thus losing the terror of separateness. When Christianity and Islam, five hundred and one thousand years later, respectively, carried the same idea to Europe and the Mediterranean countries, a large part of the world had learned the new message. But as soon as man had heard the message he began to falsify it; instead of becoming fully human himself, he idolized God and dogmas as manifestations of the "new goal," thus substituting a figure or a word for the reality of his own experience. And yet again and again man tried also to return to the authentic aim; such attempts manifested themselves within religion, in heretic sects, in new philosophical thoughts and political philosophies.

Different as the thought concepts of all these new religions and movements are, they have in common the idea of the basic alternative of man. Man can choose only between two possibilities: to regress or to move forward. He can either return to an archaic, pathogenic solution, or he can progress toward, and develop, his humanity. We find the formulation of this alternative in various ways; as the alternative between light and darkness (Persia); between blessing and curse, life and death (the Old Testament); or the socialist formulation of the alternative between socialism and barbarism.

The same alternative is presented not only by the various humanist religions, but it appears also as the basic difference between mental health and mental illness. What we call a healthy person depends on the general frame of reference of a given culture. With the Teutonic Berserks a "healthy" man would have been one who was capable of acting like a wild animal. The same man would be a psychotic today. All archaic forms of mental experience—necrophilia, extreme narcissism, incestuous symbiosis—which in one form or the other have constituted the "normal" or even the "ideal" in regressive-archaic cultures because men were united by their common archaic strivings are today designated as severe forms of mental pathology. In a less intense form, when opposed by contrary forces, these archaic forces are repressed, and the result of this repression is a "neurosis." The essential difference between the archaic orientation in a regressive and in a progressive culture, respectively, lies in the fact that the archaically oriented person in an archaic culture does not feel isolated but, on the contrary, is supported by the common consensus, while the opposite is true for the same person in a progressive culture. He "loses his mind" because his mind is in opposition to that of all others. The fact is that even in a progressive culture such as today's, a large number of its members have regressive tendencies of considerable strength, but they are repressed in the normal course of life and become manifest only under special conditions, such as war.

Let us sum up what these considerations tell us about the questions with which we started. First of all, as to the question of the nature of man, we arrive at the conclusion that the nature or essence of man is not a specific *substance,* like good or evil, but a *contradiction* which is rooted in the very conditions of human existence. This conflict in itself requires a solution, and basically there are only the regressive or the progressive solutions. What has sometimes appeared as an innate drive for progress in man is nothing other than the dynamics of a search for new solutions. At any new level man has reached new contradictions appear which force him to go on with the task of finding new solutions. This process goes on until he has reached the final goal of becoming fully human and being in complete union with the world. Whether man can reach this final goal of full "awakening" in which greed and conflict have disappeared (as Buddhism teaches) or whether this is possible only after death (according to the Christian teaching) is not our concern here. What matters is that in all humanist religions and philosophical teachings, the "New Goal" is the same, and man lives by the faith that he can achieve an ever increasing approximation to it. (On the other hand, if solutions are sought for in a regressive way, man will be bound to seek for complete dehumanization which is the equivalent of madness.)

If the essence of man is neither the good nor the evil, neither love nor hate, but a contradiction which demands the search for new solutions which, in turn, create new contradictions, then indeed man can answer his dilemma, either in a regressive or in a progressive way. Recent history gives us many examples for this. Millions of Germans, especially those of the lower middle class, who had lost money and social status reverted under the leadership of Hitler to their teutonic ancestors' cult of "going berserk." The same happened in the case of the Russians under Stalin, with the Japanese during the "rape" of Nanking, with the lynch mobs in the American South. For the majority the archaic form of experience is always a real possibility; it *can* emerge. However it is necessary to distinguish between two forms of emergence. One is when the archaic impulses remained very strong but were repressed because they were contrary to the culture patterns of a given civilization; in this case specific circumstances such as war, natural catastrophes, or social disintegration can easily open the channels, permitting the repressed archaic impulses to surge forward. The other possibility is when in the development of a person, or of the members of a group, the progressive stage had really been reached and solidified; in this case traumatic incidents like those mentioned above will not easily produce a return of the archaic impulses, because these had been not so much repressed as *replaced;* nevertheless even in this case the archaic potential has not entirely disappeared; under extraordinary circumstances such as prolonged imprisonment in concentration camps, or certain chemical processes in the body, the entire psychic system of a person may break down and the archaic forces may surge forward with renewed strength. There are, of course, innumerable shadings between the two extremes— the archaic, repressed impulses, on the one hand, and their full replacement by the progressive orientation, on the other. The proportion will be different in each person, and also the degree of repression versus the degree of awareness of the archaic orientation. There are people in whom the archaic side has been so completely eliminated, not by repression but by the development of the progressive orientation, that they may have lost the capability of even regressing to it. In the same way there are persons who have so completely destroyed all possibilities for the development of a progressive orientation that they too have lost the freedom of choice—in this case, the choice to progress.

It goes without saying that the general spirit of a given society will influence to a large extent the development of the two sides in each individual. Yet, even here individuals can differ greatly from the social pattern of orientation. As I have already pointed out, there are millions of archaically oriented individuals in modern society who consciously believe in the doctrines of Christianity or Enlightenment, yet who behind this façade are "berserks," necrophiles or worshipers of Baal or Astarte. They do not even necessarily experience any conflict, because the progressive ideas they *think* have no weight, and they *act* upon their archaic impulses only in hidden or veiled forms. On the other hand, many times there have been in archaic cultures individuals who developed a progressive orientation; they became the leaders who under certain circumstances brought light to the majority of their group, and who laid the basis for a gradual change of the entire society. When these individuals were of unusual stature, and when traces of their teachings remained, they were called prophets, masters, or some such name. Without them mankind would never have moved from the darkness of the archaic state. Yet they have been able to influence man only because in the evolution of work man liberated himself gradually from the unknown forces of nature, developed his reason and objectivity, ceased to live like an animal of prey or of burden.

What holds true of groups holds true also of individuals. In every person there is a potential of archaic forces which we have just discussed. Only the thoroughly "evil" and the thoroughly "good" no longer have a choice. Almost everybody can regress to the archaic orientation, or progress to the full progressive unfolding of his personality. In the first case we speak of the outbreak of severe mental illness; in the second case we speak of a spontaneous recovery from illness, or a transformation of the person into full awakening and maturity. It is the task of psychiatry, psychoanalysis, and various spiritual disciplines to study the conditions under which the one or the other development occurs and, furthermore, to devise methods by which the favorable development can be furthered and the malignant development stopped.[3] The description of these methods falls outside the scope of this book, and is to be found in the clinical literature of psychoanalysis and psychiatry. But it is important for our problem to recognize that, aside from the extreme cases, each individual and each group of individuals can at any given point regress to the most irrational and destructive orientations and also progress toward the enlightened and progressive orientation. Man *is* neither good nor evil. If one believes in the goodness of man as the only potentiality, one will be forced into rosy falsification of the facts, or end up in bitter disillusionment. If one believes in the other extreme, one will end up as a cynic and be blind to the many possibilities for good in others and in oneself. A realistic view sees both possibilities as real potentialities, and studies the conditions for the development of either of them.

These considerations lead us to the problem of man's *freedom*. Is man free to choose the good at any given moment, or has he no such freedom of choice because he is determined by forces inside and outside himself? Many volumes have been written on the question of freedom of will and I can find no more adequate statement as an introduction to the following pages than William James' remarks on the subject. "A common opinion

[3] Cf. especially the teachings and practice of Zen Buddhism as espoused by D. T. Suzuki in his many books. Cf. in particular D. T. Suzuki, E. Fromm, and R. de Martino, *Zen Buddhism and Psychoanalysis* (New York: Harper & Row, 1961).

prevails," he wrote, "that the juice has ages ago been pressed out of the free-will controversy, and that no new champion can do more than warm up stale arguments which everyone has heard. This is a radical mistake. I know of no subject less worn out, or in which incentive genius has a better chance of breaking open new ground—not, perhaps, of forcing a conclusion or of coercing assent, but of deepening our sense of what the issue between the two parties really is, and of what the ideas of fate and of free will really imply."[4] My attempt to present in the following pages some suggestions with regard to this problem is based on the fact that psychoanalytic experience may throw some new light on the question of freedom and thus permit us to see some new aspects.

The traditional treatment of freedom has suffered from the lack of using empirical, psychological data, and thus has led to a tendency to discuss the problem in general and abstract terms. If we mean by freedom *freedom of choice,* then the question amounts to asking whether we are free to choose between, let us say, A and B. The determinists have said that we are not free, because man—like all other things in nature—is determined by causes; just as a stone dropped in mid-air is not free *not* to fall, so man is compelled to choose A or B, because of motives determining him, forcing him, or causing him to choose A or B.[5]

The opponents of determinism claim the opposite; it is argued on religious grounds that God gave man the freedom to choose between good and evil—hence that man has this freedom. Second, it is argued that man is free since otherwise he could not be made responsible for his acts. Third, it is argued, man has the subpective experience of being free, hence this consciousness of

[4] William James, "The Dilemma of Determinism", 1884, reprinted in *A Modern Introduction to Philosophy* by Paul Edwards and Arthur Pap. New York: The Free Press, 1957.

[5] The word determinism is used here and throughout this book to refer to what William James and contemporary Anglo-Saxon philosophers mean by "hard determinism". Determinism is this sense is to be distinguished from the kind of theory found in the writings of Hume and Mill which is sometimes called "soft determinism" and according to which it is consistent to believe in determinism and in human freedom. While my position is more akin to "soft" than "hard" determinism it is not that of the former either.

freedom is a proof of the existence of freedom. All three arguments seem unconvincing. The first requires belief in God, and a knowledge of his plans for man. The second seems to be born out of the wish to make man responsible so that he can be punished. The idea of punishment, which is part of most social systems in the past and in the present, is mainly based on what is (or is considered to be) a measure of protection for the minority of "haves" against the majority of "have nots," and is a symbol of the punishing power of authority. If one wants to punish, one needs to have someone who is responsible. In this respect one is reminded of Shaw's saying, "The hanging is over—all that remains is the trial." The third argument, that the consciousness of freedom of choice proves that this freedom exists, was already thoroughly demolished by Spinoza and Leibniz. Spinoza pointed out that we have the illusion of freedom because we are aware of our desires, but unaware of their motivations. Leibniz also pointed out that the will is motivated by tendencies which are partly unconscious. It is surprising indeed, that most of the discussion after Spinoza and Leibniz has failed to recognize the fact that the problem of freedom of choice cannot be solved unless one considers that unconscious forces determine us, though leaving us with the happy conviction that our choice is a free one. But aside from these specific objections, the arguments for the freedom of will seem to contradict everyday experience; whether this position is held by religious moralists, idealistic philosophers, or Marxist-leaning existentialists, it is at best a noble postulate, and yet perhaps not such a noble one, because it is deeply unfair to the individual. Can one really claim that a man who has grown up in material and spiritual poverty, who has never experienced love or concern for anybody, whose body has been conditioned to drinking by years of alcoholic abuse, who has had no possibility of changing his circumstances—can one claim that he is "free" to make his choice? Is not this position contrary to the facts; and is it not without compassion and, in the last analysis, a position which in the language of the twentieth century reflects, like much of Sartre's philosophy, the spirit of bourgeois individualism and egocentricity, a modern version of

Max Stirner's *Der Einzige und sein Eigentum* (The Unique One and His Property)?

The opposite position, determinism, which postulates that man is *not* free to choose, that his decisions are at any given point caused and determined by external and internal events which have occurred before, appears at first glance more realistic and rational. Whether we apply determinism to social groups and classes or to individuals, have not Freudian and Marxist analysis shown how weak man is in his battle against determining instinctive and social forces? Has not psychoanalysis shown that a man who has never solved his dependency on his mother lacks the ability to act and to decide, that he feels weak and thus is forced into an ever increasing dependency on mother figures, until he reaches the point of no return? Does not Marxist analysis demonstrate that once a class—such as the lower middle class—has lost fortune, culture, and a social function, its members lose hope and regress to archaic, necrophilic, and narcissistic orientations?

Yet neither Marx nor Freud were determinists in the sense of believing in an irreversibility of causal determination. They both believed in the possibility that a course already initiated can be altered. They both saw this possibility of change rooted in man's capacity for *becoming aware of the forces which move him* behind his back, so to speak—and thus enabling him to regain his freedom.[6] Both were—like Spinoza, by whom Marx was influenced considerably—determinists *and* indeterminists, or neither determinists *nor* indeterminists. Both proposed that man is determined by the laws of cause and effect, but that by awareness and right action he can create and enlarge the realm of freedom. It is up to him to gain an optimum of freedom and to extricate himself from the chains of necessity. For Freud the awareness of the unconscious, for Marx the awareness of socio-economic forces and class interests, were the conditions for liberation; for both, in

---

[6] Cf. a more detailed discussion of this point in E. Fromm, *Beyond the Chains of Illusion*, New York: Simon and Schuster, 1962, and Pocket Books, Inc., New York, 1963.

addition to awareness, an active will and struggle were necessary conditions for liberation.[7]

Certainly every psychoanalyst has seen patients who have been able to reverse the trends which seemed to determine their lives, once they became aware of them and made a concentrated effort to regain their freedom. But one need not be a psychoanalyst to have this experience. Some of us have had the same experience either with ourselves or with other people: the chain of *alleged* causality was broken and they took a course which seemed "miraculous" because it contradicted the most reasonable expectations that could have been formed on the basis of their past performances.

The traditional discussion on freedom of will has suffered not only from the fact that Spinoza's and Leibniz's discovery of unconscious motivation did not find its proper place. There are also other reasons which are responsible for the seeming futility of the discussion. In the following paragraphs I shall mention some of the errors which, in my opinion, have a major importance.

One error lies in the habit of speaking of the freedom of choice of *man* rather than that of a specific individual.[8] I shall try to show later that as soon as one speaks of the freedom of man in general, rather than of an individual, one speaks in an abstract way which makes the problem insoluble; this is so precisely because one man has the freedom to choose—another has lost it. If applied to all men, we either deal with an abstraction, or with

[7] Basically the same position is taken by classic Buddhism. Man is chained to the wheel of rebirth, yet he can liberate himself from this determinism by awareness of his existential situation and by walking along the eightfold path of right action. The Old Testament prophets' position is similar. Man has the choice between "blessing and curse, life and death" but he may arrive at a point of no return if he hesitates too long in choosing life.

[8] This error is to be found even in a writer, Austin Farrar, whose writings on freedom belong to the most subtle, penetrating, and objective analyses of freedom. He writes: "Choice, by definition, lies between alternatives. That an alternative is genuinely and psychologically open to choice can be supported by *the observation that people have chosen it.* That people have sometimes failed to choose it, has no tendency to show that it is closed to choice" (*The Freedom Of The Will* [London: A. and C. Black, 1958], p. 151, my emphasis, E. F.).

a mere moral postulate in the sense of Kant or of William James. Another difficulty in the traditional discussion of freedom seems to lie in the tendency, especially of the classic authors from Plato to Aquinas, to deal with the problem of good and evil in a general way, as if man had the choice between good and evil "in general," and the freedom to choose the good. This view greatly confuses the discussion because, when confronted with the general choice most men choose "good" as against "evil." But there is no such thing as the choice between "good" and "evil"—there are concrete and specific actions that are *means* toward what is good, and others that are means toward what is evil, provided good and evil are properly defined. Our moral conflict on the question of choice arises when we have to make a concrete decision rather than when we choose good or evil in general.

Still another shortcoming of the traditional discussion lies in the fact that it usually deals with freedom versus determinism of choice, rather than with various degree of inclinations.[9] As I shall try to show later, the problem of freedom versus determinism is really one of conflict of inclinations and their respective intensities.

Finally, there is confusion in the use of the concept of "responsibility." "Responsibility" is mostly used to denote that I am punishable or accusable; in this respect it makes little difference whether I permit others to accuse me or whether I accuse myself. If I find myself guilty, I punish myself; if others find me guilty, they will punish me. There is another concept of responsibility, however, which has no connection with punishment or "guilt." In this sense responsibility only means "I am aware that I did it." In fact, as soon as my deed is experienced as "sin" or "guilt" it becomes alienated. It is not *I* who did this, but "the sinner," "the bad one," that "other person" who now needs to be punished; not to speak of the fact that the feeling of guilt and self-accusation creates sadness, self-loathing, and loathing of life. This point has been beautifully expressed by one of the great Hasidic teachers, Isaac Meier of Ger:

[9] Leibniz is one of the relatively few authors who speak about *"incliner sans necessiter."*

Whoever talks about and reflects upon an evil thing he has done, is thinking the vileness he has perpetrated, and what one thinks, therein is one caught—with one's whole soul one is caught utterly in what one thinks, and so he is still caught in vileness. And he will surely not be able to turn, for his spirit will coarsen and his heart rot, and besides this, a sad mood may come upon him. What would you? Stir filth this way and that, and it is still filth. To have sinned or not to have sinned —what does it profit us in heaven? In the time I am brooding on this, I could be stringing pearls for the joy of heaven. That is why it is written: "Depart from evil, and do good"—turn wholly from evil, do not brood in its way, and do good. You have done wrong? Then balance it by doing right.[10]

It is in the same spirit that the Old Testament word *chatah*, usually translated as meaning "sin," actually means "to miss" (the road); it lacks the quality of condemnation which the words "sin" and "sinner" have. Similarly, the Hebrew word for "repentence" is *teschubah*, meaning "return" (to God, to oneself, to the right way), and it also lacks the implication of self-condemnation. Thus the Talmud uses the expression "the master of return" ("the repentent sinner") and says of him that he stands even above those who have never sinned.

Assuming we agree that we speak of the freedom of choice between two specific courses of action which one specific individual is confronted with, then we might begin our discussion with one concrete, commonplace example: the freedom of choice between smoking or not smoking. Let us take a heavy smoker who has read the reports on the health hazards of smoking and has arrived at the conclusion that he wants to stop smoking. He has "decided that he is going to stop." This "decision" is no decision. It is nothing but the formulation of a hope. He has "decided" to stop smoking, yet the next day he feels in too good a mood, the day after in too bad a mood, the third day he does not want to appear "asocial," the following day he doubts that the health reports are correct, and so he continues smoking, although he had "decided" to stop. All these decisions are nothing but ideas, plans, fantasies; they have little or no reality until the real

---

[10] Quoted in *In Time and Eternity*, ed. by N. N. Glatzer (New York: Schocken Books, 1946), p. 00.

choice is made. This choice becomes real when he has a cigarette in front of him and has to decide whether to smoke *this* cigarette or not; again, later he has to decide about another cigarette, and so on. It is always the concrete act which requires a decision. The question in each such situation is whether he is free not to smoke, or whether he is not free.

Several questions arise here. Assuming he did not believe in the health reports on smoking or, even if he did, he is convinced that it is better to live twenty years less than to miss this pleasure; in this case there is apparently no problem of choice. Yet the problem may only be camouflaged. His conscious thoughts may be nothing but rationalizations of his feeling that he could not win the battle even if he tried; hence he may prefer to pretend that there is no battle to win. But whether the problem of choice is conscious or unconscious, the nature of the choice is the same. It is the choice between an action which is dictated by reason as against an action which is dictated by irrational passions. According to Spinoza, freedom is based on "adequate ideas" which are based on the awareness and acceptance of reality and which determine actions securing the fullest development of the individual's psychic and mental unfolding. Human action, according to Spinoza, is causally determined by passions or by reason. When ruled by passions, man is in bondage; when by reason, he is free.

Irrational passions are those which overpower man and compel him to act contrary to his true self-interests, which weaken and destroy his powers and make him suffer. The problem of freedom of choice is *not* that of choosing between two equally good possibilities; it is not the choice between playing tennis or going on a hike, or between visiting a friend or staying at home reading. The freedom of choice where determinism or indeterminism is involved is always the freedom to choose the *better* as against the worse—and better or worse always is understood in reference to the basic moral question of life—that between progressing or regressing, between love and hate, between independence and dependence. Freedom is nothing other than the capacity to follow the voice of reason, of health, of well-being, of conscience, against the voices of irrational passions. In this respect we agree with the traditional views of Socrates, Plato, the Stoics, Kant. What I am trying to emphasize is that the freedom to follow the commands of reason is a psychological problem that can be examined further.

Let us return to our example of the man who is confronted with the choice of either smoking or not smoking this cigarette or, to put it differently, to the problem of whether he has the *freedom* to follow his rational intention. We can imagine an individual of whom we can predict with near certainty that he will not be able to follow his intention. Assuming he is a man deeply bound to a mothering figure and with an oral-receptive orientation, a man who is always expecting something from others, who has never been able to assert himself, and because of all this is filled with intense and chronic anxiety; smoking, to him, is the satisfaction of his receptive craving, and a defense against his anxiety; the cigarette, to him, symbolizes strength, adultness, activity, and for this reason he cannot do without it. His craving for the cigarette is the result of his anxiety, his receptiveness, etc., and is as strong as these motives are. There is a point where they are so strong that the person would not be able to overcome his craving unless some drastic change were to occur in the balance of forces within him. Otherwise we can say that he is, for all practical purposes, not free to choose what he has recognized to be the better. On the other hand, we may imagine a man of such maturity, productivity, lack of greed, that he would not be able to act in a way that is contrary to reason and to his true interests. He also would not be "free"; he could not smoke because he would feel no inclination to do so.[11]

Freedom of choice is not a formal abstract capacity which one either "has" or "has not"; it is, rather, a function of a person's character structure. Some people have no freedom to choose the good because their character structure has lost the capacity to act in accordance with the good. Some people have lost the capacity of choosing the evil, precisely because their character

[11] St. Augustine speaks of the state of beatitude in which man is not free to sin.

structure has lost the craving for evil. In these two extreme cases we may say that both are determined to act as they do because the balance of forces in their character leaves them no choice. In the majority of men, however, we deal with contradictory inclinations which are so balanced that a choice *can* be made. The act is the result of the respective strength of conflicting inclinations within the person's character.

It must be clear by now that we can use the concept "freedom" in two different senses: In one, freedom is an attitude, an orientation, part of the character structure of the mature, fully developed, productive person; in this sense I can speak of a "free" person as I can speak of a loving, productive, independent person. In fact, a free person in this sense *is* a loving, productive, independent person; freedom in this sense has no reference to a special choice between two possible actions, but to the character structure of the person involved; and in this sense the person who "is not free to choose evil" is the completely free person. The second meaning of freedom is the one which we have mainly used so far, namely, the capacity to make a choice between opposite alternatives; alternatives which, however, always imply the choice between the rational and the irrational interest in life and its growth versus stagnation and death; when used in this second sense the best and the worst man are not free to choose, while it is precisely the average man with contradictory inclinations, for whom the problem of freedom of choice exists.

If we speak of freedom in this second sense the question arises: On what factors does this freedom to choose between contradictory inclinations depend?

Quite obviously the most important factor lies in the respective strengths of the contradictory inclinations, particularly in the strength of the unconscious aspects of these inclinations. But if we ask what factors support freedom of choice even if the irrational inclination is stronger, we find that the decisive factor in choosing the better rather than the worse lies in *awareness*. (1) awareness of what constitutes good or evil; (2) which action in the concrete situation is an appropriate means to the desired end; (3) awareness of the forces behind the apparent

wish; that means the discovery of _unconscious_ desires; (4) awareness of the real possibilities between which one can choose; (5)
awareness of the consequences of the one choice as against the
other; (6) awareness of the fact that awareness as such is not
effective unless it is accompanied by the _will_ to act, by the readiness to suffer the pain of frustration that necessarily results from
an action contrary to one's passions.

Let us now examine these various kinds of awareness. _Aware-
ness_ of what is good and evil is different from theoretical _knowl-
edge_ of what is called good and evil in most moral systems. To
know on the authority of tradition that love, independence, and
courage are good and that hate, submission, and cowardice are
bad means little, as the knowledge is alienated knowledge learned
from authorities, conventional teaching, etc., and is believed to
be true only because it comes from these sources. Awareness
means that the person makes that which he learns his own, by
experiencing it, experimenting with himself, observing others
and, eventually, gaining a conviction rather than having an
irresponsible "opinion." But deciding on the general principles
is not enough. Beyond this awareness one needs to be aware of
the balance of forces within oneself, and the rationalizations
which hide the unconscious forces.

Let us take a specific example: A man is greatly attracted by a
woman and experiences a strong wish to have sexual intercourse
with her. He thinks consciously that he has this wish because
she is so beautiful, or so understanding, or so in need of being
loved, or that he is so sexually starved, or so in need of affection,
or so lonely, or . . . He may be aware that by having an affair
with her he might mess up both their lives; that she is frightened
and seeking for protective strength, and hence will not easily let
him go. In spite of knowing all this he goes ahead and has an
affair with her. Why? Because he is aware of his desire, but not
of the forces underlying it. What could these forces be? I shall
mention only one among a number, although one which is
frequently very effective: his vanity and narcissism. If he has set
his mind on the conquest of this girl as a proof of his attractive-
ness and value he will usually not be aware of this real motive.

He will fall for all the rationalizations mentioned above, and many more, and thus act according to his true motive precisely because he cannot see it, and is under the illusion that he is acting according to other more reasonable motives.

The next step of awareness is that of the full awareness of the *consequences* of his act. At the moment of decision his mind is filled with desires and soothing rationalization. His decision, however, might be different if he could clearly see the consequences of his act; if he could see, for instance, a long-protracted, insincere love affair, his getting tired of her because his narcissism can be satisfied only by fresh conquests, yet his continuing to make false promises because he feels guilty and afraid of admitting that he never really loved her, the paralyzing and weakening effect of this conflict on him and on her, etc.

But even awareness of the underlying, real motivations and of the consequences is not enough to increase the inclination for the right decision. Another important awareness is necessary: that of *when* the real choice is made, and to be aware of what the real possibilities are between which a person can choose.

Assume he is aware of all motivations and of all consequences; assume he has "decided" not to go to bed with this woman. He then takes her out to a show and before taking her home he suggests, "Let's have a drink together." On the face of it this sounds harmless enough. There seems to be nothing wrong in having a drink together; in fact, there would be nothing wrong if the balance of forces were not already so delicate. If at that moment he could be aware of what "having a drink together" will lead to, he might not ask her. He would see that the atmosphere will be romantic, that the drink will weaken his willpower, that he will not be able to resist the next step of dropping into her apartment for another drink, and that almost certainly he will find himself making love to her. With full awareness he would be able to foresee the sequence as being almost unavoidable, and if he could foresee it, he could refrain from "having a drink together." But since his desire makes him blind to seeing the necessary sequence, he does not make the right choice when he still would have the possibility of doing so. In other words, the real choice here is made when he invites her to have a drink (or perhaps when he asked her to the show) and not when he starts making love to her. At the last point of the chain of decisions he is no longer free; at an earlier point he might have been free had he been aware that the real decision was to be made right there and then. The argument for the view that man has no freedom to choose the better as against the worse is to some considerable extent based on the fact that one looks usually at the *last* decision in a chain of events, and not at the first or second ones. Indeed, at the point of final decision the freedom to choose has usually vanished. But it may still have been there at an earlier point when the person was not yet so deeply caught in his own passions. One might generalize by saying that one of the reasons why most people fail in their lives is precisely because they are not aware of the point when they are still free to act according to reason, and because they are aware of the choice only at the point when it is too late for them to make a decision.

Closely related to the problem of seeing when the real decision is made is another one. Our capacity to choose changes constantly with our practice of life. The longer we continue to make the wrong decisions, the more our heart hardens; the more often we make the right decision, the more our heart softens— or better perhaps, becomes alive.

A good illustration of the principle involved here is the game of chess. Assuming that two equally skilled players begin a game, both have the same chance of winning (with a slightly better chance for the white side, which we can ignore for our purposes here); in other words, each has the same freedom to win. After, say, five moves the picture is already different. Both still *can* win, but A, who has made a better move, already has a greater chance of winning. He has, as it were, more freedom to win than his opponent, B. Yet B is still free to win. After some more moves, A, having continued to make correct moves that were not effectively countered by B, is almost sure to win, but only *almost*. B *can* still win. After some further moves the game is decided. B, provided he is a skilled player, recognizes that he has no longer the freedom to win; he sees that he has already lost before he is actually checkmated. Only the poor player who cannot properly analyze the determining factors lives under the illusion that he can still win after he has lost the freedom to do so; because of this illusion he has to go on to the bitter end, and have his king checkmated.[12]

The implication of the analogy of the chess game is obvious. Freedom is not a constant attribute which we either "have" or "have not." In fact, there is no such thing as "freedom" except as a word and an abstract concept. There is only one reality: the *act* of freeing ourselves in the process of making choices. In this process the degree of our capacity to make choices varies with each act, with our practice of life. Each step in life which increases my self-confidence, my integrity, my courage, my conviction also increases my capacity to choose the desirable alternative, until eventually it becomes more difficult for me to choose the undesirable rather than the desirable action. On the other hand, each act of surrender and cowardice weakens me, opens the path for more acts of surrender, and eventually freedom is lost. Between the extreme when I can no longer do a wrong act and the other extreme when I have lost my freedom to right action, there are innumerable degrees of freedom of choice. In the practice of life the degree of freedom to choose is different at any given moment. If the degree of freedom to choose the good is great, it needs less effort to choose the good. If it is small, it takes a great effort, help from others, and favorable circumstances.

A classic example of this phenomenon is the biblical story of Pharaoh's reaction to the demand to let the Hebrews go. He is afraid of the increasingly severe suffering brought upon him and his people; he promises to let the Hebrews go; but as soon

---

[12] The outcome may not be so bitter if it is the loss of a game of chess. But when it is the death of millions of human beings, because the generals have not the skill and objectivity to see when they have lost, the end is bitter indeed. Yet we have twice witnessed in this century such a bitter end; first in 1917, then in 1943. Both times German generals did not understand that they had lost the freedom to win, but continued the war senselessly, sacrificing millions of lives.

as the imminent danger disappears, *"his heart hardens"* and he again decides not to set the Hebrews free. This process of the hardening of the heart is the central issue in Pharaoh's conduct. The longer he refuses to choose the right, the harder his heart becomes. No amount of suffering changes this fatal development, and finally it ends in his and his people's destruction. He never underwent a *change* of heart, because he decided only on the basis of fear; and because of this lack of change, his heart became ever harder until there was no longer any freedom of choice left him.

The story of Pharaoh's hardening of heart is only the poetic expression of what we can observe every day if we look at our own development and that of others. Let us look at an example: A white boy of eight has a little friend, the son of a colored maid. Mother does not like him to play with a little Negro, and tells her son to stop seeing him. The child refuses; mother promises to take him to the circus if he will obey; he gives in. This step of self-betrayal and acceptance of a bribe has done something to the little boy. He feels ashamed, his sense of integrity has been injured, he has lost self-confidence. Yet nothing irreparable has happened. Ten years later he falls in love with a girl; it is more than an infatuation; both feel a deep human bond which unites them; but the girl is from a lower class than the boy's family. His parents resent the engagement and try to dissuade him; when he remains adamant they promise him a six months' trip to Europe if he will only wait to formalize the engagement until his return; he accepts the offer. Consciously he believes that the trip will do him a lot of good—and, of course, that he will not love his girl less when he returns. But it does not turn out this way. He sees many other girls, he is very popular, his vanity is satisfied, and eventually his love and his decision to marry become weaker and weaker. Before his return he writes her a letter in which he breaks off the engagement.

When was his decision made? Not, as he thinks, on the day he writes the final letter, but on the day when he accepted his parents' offer to go to Europe. He sensed, although not consciously, that by accepting the bribe he had sold himself—and he has to deliver what he promised: the break. His behavior in Europe is not the *reason* for the break, but the mechanism through which he succeeds in fulfilling the promise. At this point he has betrayed himself again, and the effects are increased self-contempt and (hidden behind the satisfaction of new conquests, etc.) an inner weakness and lack of self-confidence. Need we follow his life any longer in detail? He ends up in his father's business, instead of studying physics, for which he has gifts; he marries the daughter of rich friends of his parents, he becomes a successful business and political leader who makes fatal decisions against the voice of his own conscience because he is afraid of bucking public opinion. His history is one of a hardening of the heart. One moral defeat makes him more prone to suffer another defeat, until the point of no return is reached. At eight he could have taken a stand and refused to take the bribe; he was still free. And maybe a friend, a grandfather, a teacher, hearing of his dilemma, might have helped him. At eighteen he was already less free; his further life is a process of decreasing freedom, until the point where he has lost the game of life. Most people who have ended as unscrupulous, hardened men, even as Hitler's or Stalin's officials, began their lives with a chance of becoming good men. A very detailed analysis of their lives might tell us what was the degree of hardening of the heart at any given moment, and when the last chance to remain human was lost. The opposite picture exists also; the first victory makes the next one easier, until choosing the right no longer requires effort.

Our example illustrates the point that most people fail in the art of living not because they are inherently bad or so without will that they cannot live a better life; they fail because they do not wake up and see when they stand at a fork in the road and have to decide. They are not aware when life asks them a question, and when they still have alternative answers. Then with each step along the wrong road it becomes increasingly difficult for them to admit that they *are* on the wrong road, often only because they have to admit that they must go back to the first wrong turn, and must accept the fact that they have wasted energy and time.

The same holds true for social and political life. Was Hitler's victory necessary? Did the German people at any point have the freedom to overthrow him? In 1929 there were factors which made the Germans inclined to move toward Nazism: the existence of an embittered and sadistic lower middle class, whose mentality had been formed between 1918 and 1923; large-scale unemployment caused by the depression of 1929; the increasing strength of the country's militaristic forces tolerated as early as in 1918 by the social-democratic leaders; the fear of anticapitalist development on the part of the leaders of heavy industry; the Communist tactics of considering the social-democrats their main enemies; the presence of a half-crazy, though gifted, opportunistic demagogue—to mention only the most important factors. On the other hand, there were strong anti-Nazi working-class parties and there were powerful trade unions; there was an anti-Nazi liberal middle class; there was a German tradition of culture and humanism. The inclining factors on both sides were balanced in such a way that in 1929 a defeat of Nazism could still have been a real possibility. The same holds true for the period before Hitler's occupation of the Rhineland; there was a conspiracy against him among some military leaders, and there was the weakness of his military establishment; it is most probable that forceful action by the Western allies would have brought about Hitler's downfall. On the other hand, what would have happened had Hitler not antagonized the populations of the occupied nations by his insane cruelty and brutality? What would have happened if he had listened to his generals, who advised strategic retreats from Moscow, Stalingrad, and other positions? Was he still free to avoid complete defeat?

Our last example leads to another aspect of awareness which determines to a large extent the capacity to choose: awareness of those alternative choices which are real as against those alternatives which are impossible because they are not based on real possibilities.

The position of determinism claims that there is in every situation of choice only one *real* possibility; the free man, according to Hegel, acts in awareness of this one possibility, that is, of necessity; the man who is not free is blind to it, and hence is forced to act in a certain way without knowing that he is the executor of necessity, that is, of reason. On the other hand, from the indeterministic standpoint there are at the moment of choice many possibilities and man is free to choose among them. However there is often not simply *one* "real possibility," but two or even more. There is never any arbitrariness which leaves man with the choice among an *unlimited* number of possibilities.

What is meant by "real possibility"? The real possibility is one which *can* materialize, considering the total structure of forces interacting in an individual or in a society. The real possibility is the opposite of the fictitious one which corresponds to the wishes and desires of man but which, given the existing circumstances, can never be realized. Man is a constellation of forces structured in a certain and ascertainable way. This particular structure pattern, "man," is influenced by numerous factors: by environmental conditions (class, society, family) and by hereditary and constitutional conditions; studying these constitutionally given trends we can already see that they are not necessarily "causes" which determine certain "effects." A person with a constitutionally given shyness may become either overshy, retiring, passive, discouraged, or a very intuitive person, for example, a gifted poet, a psychologist, a physician. But he has no "real possibility" of becoming an insensitive, happy-go-lucky "go-getter." Whether he follows the one or the other direction depends on other factors which incline him. The same principle holds true of a person with a constitutionally given or early acquired sadistic component; in this case a person either may become a sadist or, through having fought against and overcome his sadism, may form a particularly strong mental "antibody" which makes him incapable of acting cruelly, and also makes him highly sensitive of any cruelty on the part of others or himself; he can never become a person *indifferent* to sadism.

Returning from the "real possibilities" in the field of constitutional factors to our example of the cigarette smoker, he is confronted with two real possibilities: either remaining a chain smoker or no longer smoking a single cigarette. His belief that he has the possibility of continuing to smoke, but only a few cigarettes, turns out to be an illusion. In our example of the love affair, the man has two real possibilities: either not to take the girl out or to have a love affair with her. The possibility which he thought of, that he could have a drink with her *and* not have a love affair, was unreal, considering the constellation of forces in his and her personalities.

Hitler had a real possibility of winning the war—or at least, of not losing it so disastrously—if he had not treated the conquered populations with such brutality and cruelty, if he had not been so narcissistic as never to permit strategic retreat, etc. But there were no real possibilities outside of these alternatives. To hope, as he did, that he could give vent to his destructiveness toward the conquered populations, *and* satisfy his vanity and grandiosity by never retreating, *and* threaten all other capitalist powers by the scope of his own ambitions, *and* win the war—all this was not within the gamut of real possibilities.

The same holds true for our present situation: there is a strong inclination toward war, caused by the presence of nuclear weapons on all sides and by the mutual fear and suspicion thus engendered; there is idolatry of national sovereignty; a lack of objectivity and reason in foreign policy. On the other hand, there is the wish, among the majority of the populations in both blocs, to avoid the catastrophe of nuclear destruction; there is the voice of the rest of mankind, which insists that the big powers should not involve all others in their madness; there are social and technological factors which permit the use of peaceful solutions, and which open the way to a happy future for the human race. While we have these two sets of inclining factors, there are still two real possibilities between which man can choose: that of peace by ending the nuclear arms race and the cold war; or that of war by continuing the present policy. Both possibilities are real, even if one has greater weight than the other. There is still freedom of choice. But there is no possibility that we can go on with the arms race, *and* the cold war, *and* a paranoid hate mentality, *and* at the same time avoid nuclear destruction.

In October, 1962, it seemed as if the freedom of decision had already been lost, and that the catastrophe would occur against everybody's will, except perhaps that of some mad death-lovers. On that occasion mankind was saved. An easing of tension followed in which negotiations and compromises were possible. The present time—1964—is probably the last time at which mankind will have the freedom to choose between life or destruction. If we do not go beyond superficial arrangements which symbolize good will but do not signify an insight into the given alternatives and their respective consequences, then our freedom of choice will have vanished. If mankind destroys itself it will not be because of the intrinsic wickedness of man's heart; it will be because of his inability to wake up to the realistic alternatives and their consequences. The possibility of freedom lies precisely in recognizing which are the real possibilities between which we can choose, and which are the "unreal possibilities" that constitute our wishful thoughts whereby we seek to spare ourselves the unpleasant task of making a decision between alternatives that are real but unpopular (individually or socially). The unreal possibilities are, of course, no possibilities at all; they are pipe-dreams. But the unfortunate fact is that most of us, when confronted with the *real* alternatives and with the necessity of making a choice that requires insight and sacrifices, prefer to think that there are other possibilities that can be pursued; we thus blind ourselves to the fact that these unreal possibilities do not exist, and that their pursuit is a smoke-screen behind which fate makes its own decision. Living under the illusion that the nonpossibilities will materialize, man is then surprised, indignant, hurt, when the choice is made *for* him and the unwanted catastrophe occurs. At that point he falls into the mistaken posture of accusing others, defending himself, and/or praying to God, when the only thing he should blame is his own lack of courage to face the issue, and his lack of reason in understanding it.

We conclude, then, that man's actions are always caused by inclinations rooted in (usually unconscious) forces operating in his personality. If these forces have reached a certain intensity they may be so strong that they not only incline man but determine him—hence he has no freedom of choice. In those cases where contradictory inclinations effectively operate within the personality there is freedom of choice. This freedom is limited by the existing real possibilities. These real possibilities are *determined* by the total situation. Man's freedom lies in his possibility to choose between the existing real possibilities (alternatives). Freedom in this sense can be defined not as "acting in the awareness of necessity" but as acting on *the basis of the awareness of alternatives and their consequences.* There is never indeterminism; there is sometimes determinism, and sometimes alternativism based on the uniquely human phenomenon: awareness. To put it differently, every event is caused. But in the constellation previous to the event there may be several motivations which *can* become the cause of the next event. Which of these possible causes becomes an effective cause may depend on man's awareness of the very moment of decision. In other words, nothing is uncaused, but not everything is determined (in the "hard" meaning of the word).

The view of determinism, indeterminism, and alternativism developed here essentially follows the thought of three thinkers: Spinoza, Marx, and Freud. All three are often called "determinists." There are good reasons for doing so, the best being that they have said so themselves. Spinoza wrote: "In the mind there is no absolute or free will; but the mind is determined to wish this or that by a cause, which also has been determined by a cause, and this last by another cause and so on to infinity."[13] Spinoza explained the fact that we subjectively experience our will as free—which for Kant as for many other philosophers was the very proof of the freedom of our will—as the result of self-deception: we are aware of our desires but we are not aware of the motives of our desires. Hence we believe in the "freedom" of our desires. Freud also expressed a deterministic position; belief in psychic freedom and choice; he said indeterminism "is quite unscientific. . . . It must give way before the claims of a determinism which governs even mental life." Marx also seems

[13] *Ethic*, II, Prop. XLVIII.

to be a determinist. He discovered *laws* of history which explain political events as results of class stratification and class struggles, and the latter as the result of the existing productive forces and their development. It seems that all three thinkers deny human freedom and see in man the instrument of forces which operate behind his back, and not only incline him but determine him to act as he does. In this sense Marx would be a strict Hegelian for whom the awareness of the necessity is the maximum of freedom.[14]

Not only have Spinoza, Marx, and Freud expressed themselves in terms which seem to qualify them as determinists; many of their pupils have also understood them in this way. This holds particularly true for Marx and Freud. Many "Marxists" have talked as if there were an unalterable course of history, that the future was determined by the past, that certain events had necessarily to happen. Many of Freud's pupils have claimed the same point of view for Freud; they argue that Freud's psychology is a scientific one, precisely because it can predict effects from foregoing causes.

But this interpretation of Spinoza, Marx, and Freud as determinists entirely leaves out the other aspect in the philosophy of the three thinkers. Why was it that the main work of the "determinist" Spinoza is a book on ethics? That Marx's main intention was the socialist revolution, and that Freud's main aim was a therapy which would cure the mentally sick person of his neurosis?

The answer to these questions is simple enough. All three thinkers saw the degree to which man and society are inclined to act in a certain way, often to such a degree that the inclination becomes determination. But at the same time they were not only philosophers who wanted to explain and interpret; they were men who wanted to change and to transform. For Spinoza the task of man, his ethical aim, is precisely that of reducing determination and achieving the optimum of freedom.

[14] For a detailed discussion of these points, cf. E. Fromm, *Beyond the Chains of Illusion* (New York: Simon and Schuster, 1962, and Pocket Books 1963).

Man can do this by self-awareness, by transforming passions, which blind and chain him, into actions ("active affects"), which permit him to act according to his real interest as a human being. "An emotion which is a passion ceases to be a passion as soon as we form a distinct and clear picture thereof."[15] Freedom is not anything which is *given* to us, according to Spinoza; it is something which within certain limitations we can acquire by insight and by effort. We have the alternative to choose if we have fortitude and awareness. The conquest of freedom is difficult and that is why most of us fail. As Spinoza wrote at the end of the *Ethic*:

> I have thus completed all I wished to set forth touching the mind's power over the emotions and the mind's freedom. Whence it appears how potent is the wise man and how much he surpasses the ignorant man who is driven only by his lusts. For the ignorant man is not only distracted in various ways by external causes without ever gaining the true acquiescence of his spirit, but moreover lives, as it were, unwitting of himself, and of God, and of things, and as soon as he ceases to suffer [in Spinoza's sense, to be passive], ceases also to be.
>
> Whereas the wise man, in as far as he is regarded as such, is scarcely at all disturbed in spirit, but, being conscious of himself, and of God, and of things, by a certain eternal necessity, never ceases to be, but always possesses true acquiescence of his spirit.
>
> If the way which I have pointed out as leading to this result, seems exceedingly hard, it may nevertheless be discovered. Needs must it be hard, since it is so seldom found. How would it be possible, if salvation were ready to our hand, and could without great labour be found, that it should be by almost all men neglected? But all things excellent are as difficult as they are rare.[16]

Spinoza, the founder of modern psychology, who sees the factors which determine man, nevertheless writes an *Ethic*. He wanted to show how man can change from bondage to freedom. And his concept of "ethic" is precisely that of the conquest of freedom. This conquest is possible by reason, by adequate ideas, by awareness, but it is possible only if man makes the effort with more labor than most men are willing to make.

If Spinoza's work is a treatise aiming at the "salvation" of the

---

15 *Ethic*, V, Prop. III. loc. cit.
16 *Ibid.*, Prop. XLII, note.

individual (salvation meaning the conquest of freedom by awareness and labor), Marx's intent is also the salvation of the individual. But while Spinoza deals with individual irrationality,
Marx extends the concept. He sees that the irrationality of the
individual is caused by the irrationality of the society in which
he lives, and that this irrationality itself is the result of the
planlessness and the contradictions inherent in the economic and
social reality. Marx's aim, like Spinoza's, is the free and independent man, but in order to achieve this freedom man must become
aware of those forces which act behind his back and determine
him. Emancipation is the result of awareness and effort. More
specifically, Marx, believing that the working class was the historical agent for universal human liberation, believed that class-
consciousness and struggle were the necessary conditions for
man's emancipation. Like Spinoza, Marx is a determinist in the
sense of saying: If you remain blind and do not make the utmost
efforts, you will lose your freedom. But he, like Spinoza, is not
only a man who wants to interpret; he is a man who wants to
change—hence his whole work is the attempt to teach man how
to become free by awareness and effort. Marx never said, as is
often assumed, that he predicted historical events which would
necessarily occur. He was always an alternativist. Man can break
the chains of necessity *if* he is aware of the forces operating
behind his back, *if* he makes the tremendous effort to win his
freedom. It was Rosa Luxemburg, one of the greatest interpreters
of Marx, who formulated this alternativism thus: that in this
century man has the alternative of choosing "between socialism
and barbarism."

  Freud, the determinist, was also a man who wanted to transform: he wanted to change neurosis into health, to substitute
the dominance of the Ego for that of the Id. What else is neurosis
—of whatever kind—but man's loss of freedom to act rationally?
What else is mental health but man's capacity to act according
to his true interest? Freud, like Spinoza and Marx, saw to what
degree man is determined. But Freud also recognized that the
compulsion to act in certain irrational and thus destructive
ways can be changed—by self-awareness and by effort. Hence

his work is the attempt to devise a method of curing neurosis by self-awareness, and the motto of his therapy is: "The truth shall make you free."

Several main concepts are common to all three thinkers: (1) Man's actions are determined by previous causes, but he can liberate himself from the power of these causes by awareness and effort. (2) Theory and practice cannot be separated. In order to achieve "salvation," or freedom, one must know, one must have the right "theory." But one cannot know unless one acts and struggles.[17] It was precisely the great discovery of all three thinkers that theory and practice, interpretation and change are inseparable. (3) While they were determinists in the sense that man *can* lose the battle for independence and freedom, they were essentially alternativists: they taught that man can choose between certain ascertainable possibilities and that it depends on man which of these alternatives will occur; it depends on him as long as he has not yet lost his freedom. Thus Spinoza did not believe that every man would achieve salvation, Marx did not believe that socialism *had* to win, nor did Freud believe that every neurosis could be cured by his method. In fact, all three men were skeptics and simultaneously men of deep faith. For them freedom was more than acting in the awareness of necessity; it was man's great chance to choose the good as against the evil—it was a chance of choosing between real possibilities on the basis of awareness and effort. Their position was neither determinism nor indeterminism; it was a position of realistic, critical humanism.[18]

This is also the basic position of Buddhism. The Buddha recognized the cause of human suffering—greed. He confronts

[17] Freud, for instance, believed it to be necessary that the patient make an economic sacrifice by paying for his treatment, and the sacrifice of frustration by not acting out his irrational fantasies in order to achieve a cure.

[18] The position of alternativism described here is essentially that of the Hebrew Bible. God does not interfere in man's history by changing his heart. He sends his messengers, the prophets, with a threefold mission: to show man certain goals, to show him the consequences of his choices, and to protest against the wrong decision. It is up to man to make his choice; nobody, not even God, can "save" him. The clearest expression of this principle is expressed in God's answer to Samuel when the Hebrews wanted a king: "Now

man with the choice between the alternative of retaining his greed, suffering, and remaining chained to the wheel of rebirth, or of renouncing greed and thus ending suffering and rebirth. Man can choose between these two real possibilities: there is no other possibility available to him.

We have examined man's heart, its inclination for good and evil. Have we reached ground that is more solid than we were on when we raised some questions in the first chapter of this book?

Perhaps; at least it may be worthwhile to sum up the results of our inquiry.

1. Evilness is a specifically *human* phenomenon. It is the attempt to regress to the pre-human state, and to eliminate that which is specifically human: reason, love, freedom. Yet evilness is not only human, but tragic. Even if man regresses to the most archaic forms of experience, he can never cease being human; hence he can never be satisfied with evilness as a solution. The animal cannot be evil; it acts according to its built-in drives which essentially serve his interest for survival. Evilness is the attempt to transcend the realm of the human to the realm of the inhuman, yet it is profoundly human because man cannot become an animal as little as he can become "God." *Evil is man's loss of himself in the tragic attempt to escape the burden of his humanity.* And the potential of evil is all the greater because man is endowed with an imagination that enables him to imagine all the possibilities for evil and thus to desire and act on them, to feed his evil imagination.[19] The idea of good and evil expressed here corresponds essentially to the one expressed by

---

therefore hearken unto their voice; howbeit ye protest solemnly unto them, and show them the manner of the king that shall reign over them." After Samuel has given them a drastic description of Oriental despotism, and the Hebrews still want a king, God says: "Hearken to their voice and make them a king" (I Sam. 8:9, 22). The same spirit of alternativism is expressed in the sentence: "I put before you today blessing and curse, life and death. And you chose life." Man can choose. God cannot save him; all God can do is to confront him with the basic alternatives, life and death—and encourage him to choose life.

[19] It is interesting to note that the word for the good and evil impulse is *Jezer,* which in biblical Hebrew means "imaginings."

Spinoza. "In what follows, then," he says, "I shall mean by 'good' that which we certainly know to be a means of approaching more nearly to the type of human nature which we have set before ourselves [model of human nature, as Spinoza also calls it]; by 'bad' that which we certainly know to be a hindrance to us in approaching the said type."[20] Logically, for Spinoza, "a horse would be as completely destroyed by being changed into a man, as by being changed into an insect."[21] Good consists of transforming our existence into an ever increasing approximation to our essence; evil into an ever increasing estrangement between existence and essence.

2. The degrees of evilness are at the same time the degrees of regression. The greatest evil is those strivings which are most directed against life; the love for death, the incestuous-symbiotic striving to return to the womb, to the soil, to the inorganic; the narcissistic self-immolation which makes man an enemy of life, precisely because he cannot leave the prison of his own ego. Living this way is living in "hell."

3. There is lesser evil, according to the lesser degree of regression. There is lack of love, lack of reason, lack of interest, lack of courage.

4. Man is inclined to regress *and* to move forward; this is another way of saying he is inclined to good *and* to evil. If both inclinations are still in some balance he is free to choose, provided that he can make use of awareness and that he can make an effort. He is free to choose between alternatives which in themselves are determined by the total situation in which he finds himself. If, however, his heart has hardened to such a degree that there is no longer a balance of inclinations he is no longer free to choose. In the chain of events that lead to the loss of freedom the last decision is usually one in which man can no longer choose freely; at the first decision he may be free to choose that which leads to the good, provided he is aware of the significance of his first decision.

5. Man is responsible up to the point where he is free to

[20] *Ethic*, IV, Preface.
[21] *Ibid.*

choose for his own action. But responsibility is nothing but an ethical postulate, and often a rationalization for the authorities' desire to punish him. Precisely because evil is human, because it is the potential of regression and the loss of our humanity, it is inside every one of us. The more we are aware of it, the less are we able to set ourselves up as judges of others.

6. Man's heart can harden; it can become inhuman, yet never nonhuman. It always remains man's heart. We all are determined by the fact that we have been born human, and hence by the never-ending task of having to make choices. We must choose the means together with the aims. We must not rely on anyone's saving us, but be very aware of the fact that wrong choices make us incapable of saving ourselves.

Indeed, we must become aware in order to choose the good— but no awareness will help us if we have lost the capacity to be moved by the distress of another human being, by the friendly gaze of another person, by the song of a bird, by the greenness of grass. If man becomes indifferent to life there is no longer any hope that he can choose the good. Then, indeed, his heart will have so hardened that his "life" will be ended. If this should happen to the entire human race or to its most powerful members, then the life of mankind may be extinguished at the very moment of its greatest promise.

RELIGIOUS PERSPECTIVES

Its Meaning and Purpose

RELIGIOUS PERSPECTIVES represents a quest for the rediscovery of man. It constitutes an effort to define man's search for the essence of being in order that he may have a knowledge of goals. It is an endeavor to show that there is no possibility of achieving an understanding of man's total nature on the basis of phenomena known by the analytical method alone. It hopes to point to the false antinomy between revelation and reason, faith and knowledge, grace and nature, courage and anxiety. Mathematics, physics, philosophy, biology and religion, in spite of their almost complete independence, have begun to sense their interrelatedness and to become aware of that mode of cognition which teaches that "the light is not without but within me, and I myself am the light."

Modern man is threatened by a world created by himself. He is faced with the conversion of mind to naturalism, a dogmatic secularism and an opposition to a belief in the transcendent. He begins to see, however, that the universe is given not as one existing and one perceived but as the unity of subject and object; that the barrier between them cannot be said to have been dissolved as the result of recent experience in the physical sciences, since this barrier has never existed. Confronted with the question of meaning, he is summoned to rediscover and scrutinize the immutable and the permanent which constitute the dynamic, unifying aspect of life as well as the principle of differentiation; to reconcile identity and diversity, immutability and unrest. He begins to recognize that just as every person descends by his particular path, so he is able to ascend, and this ascent aims at a return to the source of creation, an inward home from which he has become estranged.

It is the hope of RELIGIOUS PERSPECTIVES that the rediscovery of man will point the way to the rediscovery of God. To this end a rediscovery of first principles should constitute part of the quest. These principles, not to be superseded by new discoveries, are not those of historical worlds that come to be and perish. They are to be sought in the heart and spirit of man, and no interpretation of a merely historical or scientific universe can guide the search. RELIGIOUS PERSPECTIVES attempts not only to ask dispassionately what the nature of God is, but also to restore to human life at least the hypothesis of God and the symbols that relate to him. It endeavors to show that man is faced with the metaphysical question of the truth of religion while he encounters the empirical question of its effects on the life of humanity and its meaning for society. Religion is here distinguished from theology and its doctrinal forms and is intended to denote the feelings, aspirations and acts of men, as they relate to total reality.

RELIGIOUS PERSPECTIVES is nourished by the spiritual and intellectual energy of world thought, by those religious and ethical leaders who are not merely spectators but scholars deeply involved in the critical problems common to all religions. These thinkers recognize that human morality and human ideals thrive only when set in a context of a transcendent attitude toward religion and that by pointing to the ground of identity and the common nature of being in the religious experience of man, the essential nature of religion may be defined. Thus, they are committed to re-evaluate the meaning of everlastingness, an experience which has been lost and which is the content of that *visio Dei* constituting the structure of all religions. It is the many absorbed everlastingly into the ultimate unity, a unity subsuming what Whitehead calls the fluency of God and the everlastingness of passing experience.

These volumes seek to show that the unity of which we speak consists in a certitude emanating from the nature of man who seeks God and the nature of God who seeks man. Such certitude bathes in an intuitive act of cognition, participating in the divine essence and is related to the natural spirituality of intelligence. This is not by any means to say that there is an equivalence of all faiths in the traditional religions of human history. It is, however, to emphasize the distinction between the spiritual and the temporal which all religions acknowledge. For duration of thought is composed of instants superior to time, and is an intuition of the permanence of existence and its metahistorical reality. In fact, the symbol* itself found on cover and jacket of each volume of RELIGIOUS PERSPECTIVES is the visible sign or representation of the essence, immediacy and timelessness of religious experience; the one immutable center, which may be analogically related to Being in pure act, moving with centrifugal and ecumenical necessity outward into the manifold modes, yet simultaneously, with dynamic centripetal power and with full intentional energy, returning to the source. Through the very diversity of its authors, the Series shows that the basic and poignant concern of every faith is to point to and overcome the crisis in our apocalyptic epoch—the crisis of man's separation from man and of man's separation from God—the failure of love. The authors endeavor, moreover, to illustrate the truth that the human heart is able, and even yearns, to go to the very lengths of God; that the darkness and cold, the frozen spiritual misery of recent time, are breaking, cracking and beginning to move, yielding to efforts to overcome spiritual muteness and moral paralysis. In this way, it is hoped, the immediacy of pain and sorrow, the primacy of tragedy and suffering in human life, may be transmuted into a spiritual and moral triumph. For the uniqueness of man lies in his capacity for self-transcendence.

RELIGIOUS PERSPECTIVES is therefore an effort to explore the *meaning* of God, an exploration which constitutes an aspect of man's intrinsic nature, part of his ontological substance. The Series grows out of an abiding concern that in spite of the release of man's creative energy which science has in part accomplished, this very science has overturned the essential order of nature. Shrewd as man's calculations have become concerning his means, his choice of ends which was formerly correlated with belief in God, with absolute criteria of conduct, has become witless. God is not to be treated as an exception to metaphysical principles, invoked to prevent their collapse. He is rather their

* From the original design by Leo Katz.

chief exemplification, the source of all potentiality. The personal reality of freedom and providence, of will and conscience, may demonstrate that "he who knows" commands a depth of consciousness inaccessible to the profane man, and is capable of that transfiguration which prevents the twisting of all good to ignominy. This religious content of experience is not within the province of science to bestow; it corrects the error of treating the scientific account as if it were itself metaphysical or religious; it challenges the tendency to make a religion of science—or a science of religion—a dogmatic act which destroys the moral dynamic of man. Indeed, many men of science are confronted with unexpected implications of their own thought and are beginning to accept, for instance, the trans-spatial and trans-temporal dimension in the nature of reality.

RELIGIOUS PERSPECTIVES attempts to show the fallacy of the apparent irrelevance of God in history. The Series submits that no convincing image of man can arise, in spite of the many ways in which human thought has tried to reach it, without a philosophy of human nature and human freedom which does not exclude God. This image of *Homo cum Deo* implies the highest conceivable freedom, the freedom to step into the very fabric of the universe, a new formula for man's collaboration with the creative process and the only one which is able to protect man from the terror of existence. This image implies further that the mind and conscience are capable of making genuine discriminations and thereby may reconcile the serious tensions between the secular and religious, the profane and sacred. The idea of the sacred lies in what it *is*, timeless existence. By emphasizing timeless existence against reason as a reality, we are liberated, in our communion with the eternal, from the otherwise unbreakable rule of "before and after." Then we are able to admit that all forms, all symbols in religions, by their negation of error and their affirmation of the actuality of truth, make it possible to experience that *knowing* which is above knowledge, and that dynamic passage of the universe to unending unity.

The volumes in this Series seek to challenge the crisis which separates, to make reasonable a religion that binds and to present the numinous reality within the experience of man. Insofar as the Series succeeds in this quest, it will direct mankind toward a reality that is eternal and away from a preoccupation with that which is illusory and ephemeral.

For man is now confronted with his burden and his greatness: "He calleth to me, Watchman, what of the night? Watchman, what of the night?"[1] Perhaps the anguish in the human soul may be assuaged by the answer, by the *assimilation* of the person in God: "The morning cometh, and also the night: if ye will inquire, inquire ye: return, come."[2]

RUTH NANDA ANSHEN

[1] Isaiah 21:11.
[2] *Ibid.*, 21:12.

Index

Abel, biblical story, 35
Abraham, K., 69
Adam and Eve, 19f, 35n
Adler, Alfred, 62
aggression, 13, 24n, 25; *see also* destructiveness, rage, violence
Alabama, 86
alcoholic, the, 74
alienation, 89f, 117, 119, 128
anal libido, 53ff
anal-sadistic character, 39, 53ff, 111ff, 114 (fig.)
Antigone, in Greek legend, 91
anxiety, 14, 31, 56n, 102, 131
apathy, 56f
Aquinas, Thomas, 128
Aristotle, 116
Astarte, pagan goddess, 122
Astray, Millán, Spanish general, 37ff
Augustine, St., 131n
authority, 29f, 40, 41, 103, 125
Aztecs, 33, 35

Baal, pagan god, 122
Berkowitz, Leonard: *Aggression*, 24n
Berserks, the Teutonic, 120
Bible, the, 47, 147n; *see also* Old Testament
biophilia, 13, 37, 39, 45, 52f, 113, 114 (fig.)
biophilous orientation, 38f, 44ff, 48, 51, 55, 108
blind/blindness, 41f *and* n
blood/bloodthirst, archaic, 33ff, 35, 42f, 98f, 103f, 107ff
Bollingen, Switzerland, 43
Borgia family, 66
Buddha/Buddhism, 15n, 81, 88, 118f, 121, 127n, 147f
bureaucracy, 53, 57, 59, 61, 94
Buss, Arnold H.: *The Psychology of Aggression*, 24n

Caesars, the, 66
Cain, biblical story, 27, 35
Caligula, 31, 76
Camus, Albert: *Caligula*, 31, 66n
castration fear, 62
cathexis, 62-65, 70f, 78

causality, 126f, 140, 143
cell fusion, 46
Cervantes, Miguel de, 38
change, possibility of, 126ff, 143, 147, 149
chess, game of, 135f
child, 28f, 42f, 51, 54f, 63f, 71f, 95-100, 103, 105, 107f 111f, 137
China, 118
choice: *see* free will; *see also* freedom, will
Christ/Christianity, 20f, 81, 89, 119, 121f
Church, Roman Catholic, 20, 25, 80ff, 149
class, lower middle: *see* lower middle class
clean/unclean, the, 46n, 53
Cohen, Hermann: *Die Religion der Vernunft aus den Quellen des Judentums*, 89 *and* n
Colosseum, at Rome, 32
compensatory violence, 30ff
Connolly, Cyril: *The Golden Horizon*, 38n
Copernicus, Nicholas, 84
coprophagia, 46
corpse, 42f
Corsica, 34
Coventry, 21
creativity, in man, 33, 77
criticism, sensitivity to, 70, 74f, 82
Cuba, 142

darkness, 41f
Darwin, Charles, 84
David, biblical king, 20
death/death instinct, 15, 23, 35, 37, 39, 43, 45f, 48-51, 53, 55, 103, 108ff
decay, syndrome of, 13f, 23, 37, 108-113, 114 (fig.)
defense, 25f, 27, 52, 55
dependence, 26, 29, 95-113, 126
depression, 70f, 75f, 102
destructiveness, 13, 19, 21-25, 30, 33, 46, 49, 50, 54, 56f, 62, 108ff, 112f, 115, 141
determinism, 122, 124, 126ff, 130, 139f, 143ff, 147, 149
disillusionment, 28ff
Djilas, Milovan, 34n
Dollard, J. *et al.*: *Frustration and Aggression*, 26n
Doob, L. W., 26n